NIRELLE

MEMORIES OF ESCAPE AND SURVIVAL

As Told to Her Children

By Elizabeth Silverstein

Published 2021.

Printed in the United States of America.

ISBN 978-1-950647-71-2 soft cover
ISBN 978-1-950647-74-3 hard cover

Cover Design: Brian Silverstein.

Back Cover Photos: Jasenovac Concentration Camp memorial site, Croatia. Monument, with wooden walkway created from railroad ties used to carry trains with Holocaust victims to concentration camps. Wall of names, inside memorial museum.

Publisher's Cataloging-in-Publication data

Names: Silverstein, Elizabeth, author.
Title: Nirelle : memories of WWII escape and survival as told to her children. / by Elizabeth Silverstein.
Description: First trade paperback original edition. | Parker [Colorado] : BookCrafters Publishing, 2021. | Also published in paperback.
Identifiers: ISBN 978-1-950647-74-3
Subjects: LCSH: Autobiography. | Holocaust survivors.
BISAC: BIOGRAPHY & AUTOBIOGRAPHY / Jewish.
Classification: LCC DS135.C75 2021 | DDC 940.5318092 SILVERSTEIN–dc22

Publishing assistance by BookCrafters, Parker, Colorado.
www.bookcrafters.net

Dedication

This work is dedicated to
my grandparents, Buki Alkalaj and Greta Alkalaj/Moster
and their daughter, Nirelle J. Galson

Acknowledgements

THANK YOU TO MY MOM, Nirelle Galson, for sharing her memories. Thank you to my dad, Allen Galson, for guidance, information and editing. He also patiently scanned photos while guided via a shared screen on Zoom because I could not be in his home during the Coronavirus pandemic to do the scanning myself.

My deepest gratitude goes to my husband, Paul Silverstein, for endless patience and guidance especially on historical content and for many hours of editing. Thank you to my three children who encouraged me at the beginning and came to my rescue at the end - Brian for help with the cover layout, Ilana for the Zinnia drawing and Nava for help with quotes. And, thank you to my grandson, Matthias Silverstein, for encouragement to finish the project at a moment when I stalled and for his patience while I write.

Special thank you to my siblings for their advice and edits. I am grateful for their entries as well – my sister, Deborah Galson for writing an Afterword and to my brother, Dan Galson, for writing the Foreword. Thank you to my niece, Rebecca Auron, who kindly assisted with photo scans via zoom with grandpa Allen and helped edit them afterwards for publication. Thank you to my nephews Alexander Auron and Zachary Auron for photo advice and encouragement.

I am extremely grateful to my friend Eve Madalengoitia, for weekly, sometimes daily, encouragement and editing especially in the final days of proofreading. And, thank you to our friend, Jeff Kosmacher, for his careful editing of my final copy.

I would like to acknowledge June Engel and Joyce Gutmann for their writings on the Pressburger family and their friend, Eleanor Proctor, for research on our family genealogy.

Finally, my thoughts are with my wonderful grandmothers now deceased. A special thank you to my Grandma Gertrude for inspiring me with her own written memoirs. And, I thank my Grandma Greta for sharing her memories and making us grandkids Palacsintas (Hungarian crêpes), almond crescents, and plum dumplings, when you visited Syracuse.

Table of Contents

Foreword

In 1954 my mother started a new life in the US, having recently married my American father in England, where they met while both were studying abroad. My mother is 85 now and has been living in the US for the last 66 of those years. However, it always seemed to us, her three children, that the events of her early years – growing up as a Jewish refugee in Europe and, later, in Palestine/Israel – held so much interest compared with our more mundane and peaceful upbringing in the US – that her story should be shared more widely.

From a young age we wondered about our past - our childhood was filled with exotic accents, our mother's undefinable (Croatian/Hebrew?), our grandmothers' Hungarian (mother's side) and German (father's side) - and other relatives' Portuguese (Brazil) and English (UK). These languages – and Italian too – provide the backdrop and locations of this story of survival through childhood years affected deeply by the war in Europe and the formation of the State of Israel.

This story has been written down mainly for our children and grandchildren. I hope that learning about this childhood lived under circumstances almost unimaginable today holds interest and gives insight. To her children, our mother has always been an inspiration, a source of compassion and caring, and an example of the richness and challenges to be found from going beyond perceived boundaries. But rereading this story now, I realize that I too have come to better know my Mom.

Thank you to my sister, Betsy, for the research and endeavour in tracking down and piecing together the detail of our mother's childhood story, and for the historical framing of her early life.

Daniel Galson
31 December 2020

Family Trees

ALKALAJ Family Tree (Nirelle's Father's Family)

Judah ben Solomon Chai Alkalai (1798-1878), at least one son, Juda Leon

Juda Leon Alkalaj m. Ilana (Hannah/Hana Baruch) Hannah died at Jasenovac,

Erna m. Bruno Ascoli
Daughter: Hannah (Anna) m. Bruno Servadio – three children
Daughter: Beba m. Daniel Cohen – three children
Daughter: Rachel m. Emmanuel Heller - three children
Daughter: Leah m. Ehud Shani – two children

***Buki (Mozes/Moric) m. Greta (Margit Pressburger), Buki died at Jasenovac**
***Daughter: Nirelle**
Sida m. David Baruch
Son: Micky
Son: Leon
Silvio m. Malka Ibola Avranyi (Ibi), (died at Auschwitz), Silvio died at Jasenovac
Daughter: Leonida (Leonita)(died Auschwitz)

PRESSBURGER Family Tree (Nirelle's Mother's Family)

Abraham Pressburger (d. 1896, Cefir) m. Sali Fleischhaker - at least Five children, the youngest child is Fulop, (Sali died when Fulop was 3), Abraham remarried twice.

Fulop (Phillip) PRESSBURGER m. Rosalie (Rosalia/Roza Schwartz)

Hugo died at Childbirth - first born

Zelma m. Sabetai Papo (died WWII heart attack)
Son: Philippe m. Ivanka (divorced-with no children)
M. Elaine (separated)
~ Toma (Thomas) - son, Mathias
~ Serge - two children
Daughter: Ellie m. Dalibor Bonacci (divorced)
~ Goran m. Biserka - two children, Marin and Borko
Ellie 2nd husband, Branko Knezoci (one daughter from a previous marriage)
Son: Nandi m. Terra
~ Petra
Maurice (Moritz) 1890-1918, died of Spanish Flu

Vilmos (Willy/Willhelm) 1893-1922, died of Spanish Flu/Phneumonia

Ilona m. Eugene Diosi (two children from a previous marriage: Leslie, Anna)

Son: Sandor (Sanyi) m Jutka Molnar
~ Andrew (Andris) m. Julie - two children, Debbie and Stephen
Son: Leslie (Laci) m. Marilyn
~ Michael
~ Elaine

Frederika/Frieda (Frici) m. Andor (Bandi) Revai
Daughter: June (Revai) Engel m. Norman Clare (divorced)
~ Stephanie (Steffie) m. John Kessler (divorced) - four children, Anna, Michael, Jeremy, Andrea
June 2nd husband, Raoul Engel (divorced - and no children)

Daughter: Joyce (Revai) m. James (Jim) Gutmann

Ida close relationship with Josef Strasser, who had a daughter, Edith
Edith m. Leslie Turgill -two children, Pipsi and Jane

Sari (Shari/ Sarolta) 1899-1944 m. Eugene (Jeno) Werner

Sabina 1901-1925, died from illness

***Greta (Margit) m. Buki (Mozes/Moric) Alkalaj (Alkalai) (died WWII)**
*Daughter: Nirelle (Djurdica, Guila, Judith) m. Allen Galson
~ Deborah m. Philip Auron - three children:
Zachary m. Kristen Williamson
Alexander
Rebecca
~ Daniel m. Caroline Clarke- two children:
Sam m. Madeleine Jones - daughter: Daphne Galson
Jake m. Laurie Holt
~ Elizabeth (Betsy) m. Paul Silverstein - three children:
Brian - has a son: Matthias
Ilana
Nava

Greta **2nd husband *Karl (Charles Dan) Moster** - who had a sister Mary m. Nathan (Nat) Levine

Map of Locations Mentioned, Eastern Europe

The European locations in relation to Israel

INTRODUCTION

WORLD WAR II MARCHED INTO MY MOTHER'S LIFE when she was five, old enough to have vivid memories, young enough to be among the few survivors today. I, on the other hand have never been directly impacted by any wars. In the 1960s, I remember learning to hide under our desks at school in the event of a nuclear attack. Sadly, students today are taught how to hide from a school shooter. The closest I came to experiencing war was September 11, 2001. Most people know what they were doing the day four U.S. planes were hijacked by terrorists. Two planes brought down the twin towers in NYC, one crashed into the Pentagon and one plane came down in Pennsylvania. Living in the Hudson Valley, in Poughkeepsie, NY, the last stop on the commuter train to NYC, we talked to many people impacted by 9/11. I happened to be in NYC that day, with my mother and father to attend to my mother's dying aunt. Aunt Mary was a United Nations radio correspondent in charge of the Yugoslav desk, and a survivor of WWII from Croatia. From the safety of her high-rise apartment, we watched the second tower fall and then, wearing surgical masks, walked to the yellow taped-off area to see the destruction. I'll never forget the grey dust that encrusted stores, a burned-out high-rise auto garage, the silence of NYC.

We did not see the people searching for survivors, but others living in Poughkeepsie and working in NYC were there to help rescue or traveled there to assist survivors. A few of these individuals now suffer from post-traumatic stress syndrome. The mayor of Poughkeepsie at the time lost her husband in one of the towers, a friend of mine lost her brother, a fire fighter, and my husband worked for the same company as one of the men who jumped the terrorists on United Flight 93 which crashed in a field. That was one fretful day in the United States. I can't imagine living through such events during a war which lasts for years.

As you read this, most likely, there is a war going on somewhere and people are suffering, dying, or living to share their stories and memories. Some are too painful to retell, some are about survival, and others are of everyday life. Our family, like so many other families, has its stories from our mother, father, and grandparents who lived through WWII. Their stories fascinated and intrigued us children.

My mother's memories of the war are filtered through the eyes of a child. Born in 1935 to Jewish parents, in Zagreb, Yugoslavia (now Croatia), she is lucky to be alive. In 1941, when the war arrived in Yugoslavia there were about 82,500 Jews living there. Only 14,000 of them, or 17%, survived the Holocaust. Of these, 5,000 were saved by the Italians in the area. Indeed, my mother and grandmother escaped from Yugoslavia and were eventually rescued by the Italians. My grandfather, however, and many of our extended family were victims. This memoir recounts the memories and stories my mother shared with us about her journey to safety. However, to understand my mother's childhood stories, one must also understand the history of WWII in the regions through which she fled. I have included historical references when I thought they would help understand her story.

In interviewing my mother for this manuscript, it became clear that reliving her memories was sometimes an uncomfortable task. How do you ask someone to return to a painful place in one's life, over and over, as you realize a detail needs more clarity? Do I really need to know how it felt to hear a bomb fall? Sometimes her memory faltered and that too was a hardship. Forgetting a detail that she used to remember and struggling to bring it back as her facial expression showed pain kept me from pushing too hard. Or, not knowing the answer to a question, which she herself may have always wondered about and never learned [such as, "Why did my mother leave me alone with a stranger?"] might also cause the same painful facial expression. Therefore, I let my mother lead the way, going down side roads as necessary and leaving a story for another day. There were times when my research or other family members came upon information that confirmed her memories or explained possible answers to her own questions. In those moments she found a satisfaction that healed her soul.

In our discussions, I learned that she was often asked to give a presentation of her experience. She tried to accommodate these requests, but in the end, she found the experience superficial, "not real," and declined future requests. She explains:

> *I thought the pain and sadness would just go away, but it never really goes away. The evils in the world are still here. Places like Austria and Germany that were supposedly civilized can become evil.*

For her, coming to America was a time for rebirth, if you will, a time to leave the past in the past and to focus on today and the future. Thankfully, my mother had the good fortune to do just that, and stories and questions of her past waited until she was ready to share more deeply. At one point, my mother took a writing class and wrote a few vignettes about her experience during the war using her young voice. I've included some excerpts from these stories because hearing her child's voice brings you right into the moments she describes at ages six and eight. Suddenly the story is not about my mom, or about her reflecting back, but we are right there, in the moment, with her.

When my grandmother Greta's second husband, Karl, passed away, I was sent by my parents to spend a month with her, at their apartment, in Tel Aviv, Israel. During that time, I interviewed Greta. I have a short recording of this interview. Though the quality is poor, some comments were extracted and included herein.

In 2019, as part of the research for this work, my husband Paul and I traveled on my mother's path from Zagreb to Sarajevo, Mostar, and Korčula. As such, there will be some photos and references to places we visited and people with whom we spoke.

Indented quotes are transcriptions mostly of my mother and of Greta. My mother's first name, and the one I know her as, Nirelle, is not her given name. She underwent various name changes during her early life. Within this manuscript, instead of using my mother's various names, I often just say "my mother" or "my mom." However, to be as true as possible to quotes, I leave the transcription with the name used by whomever I am quoting.

Finally, unless otherwise indicated, photo captions refer to people left to right as you view the image.

ZAGREB,YUGOSLAVIA

Greta and Buki

My mother's mother, Greta, was born Margit Miriam Pressburger in 1903, the youngest of 10 children, 7 girls and 3 boys: Zelma, Ilona, Frieda, Ida, Sari, Sabina, Greta, Maurice, Vilmos and Hugo. Hugo died in infancy. Maurice, Vilmos and Sabina died from illness as young adults.

The Pressburger Sisters
Back Row (L to R): Eugene Werner (Sari's husband), Sari, Ida, Ilona, Sabataj Papo (Zelma's husband), Zelma.
Front Row (L to R): Greta, Andor Revai (Frieda's husband), Frieda. Note: Sabina, Maurice, Vilmos, and Hugo had already died of illnesses at the time of this photo.

Greta's parents were Rosalie/Rosalia/Roza Schwartz (1862-1925) and Fulop/Phillip Pressburger (1862-1915). All ten children were born in Pressburg or Pozsony, part of the Austro-Hungarian Empire. When Pressburg became part of Czechoslovakia in 1918-19, its name changed to Bratislava. Today, Bratislava is the capital of Slovakia.

Fulop Pressburger ran a café called, *Concordia*, in Pressburg. He then moved the young family to Vienna where he opened another café catering to the artists and literati. Fulop died in 1915. So, when Greta, the youngest, was twelve, Rosalie moved the family to Budapest, Hungary, where it was less expensive to live and where she had family support. Vienna, Bratislava, and Budapest are all large cities along the Danube River. By modern travel Vienna is an hour drive to Bratislava and it is another two hours to Budapest.

My mother's father, Buki, born Mozes/Moric Alkalaj was born in 1897. He was one of four children. Buki had a brother, Sylvio (Silvio) and two sisters, Erna (Ascoli) and Sida (Baruch). Buki's parents were Leon and Hannah Alkalaj. Leon's father, Buki's grandfather, was chief rabbi of Sarajevo and of Bosnian heritage.

Greta met Buki when visiting her sister Zelma in Sarajevo, Yugoslavia. Zelma worked in a high-end crystal lighting shop. My mother fondly remembers these "shiny crystals hanging from the ceiling." The Jewish community was close and young people visited the same establishments, so perhaps they met at a party or at a bar.

Buki and Greta married on May 2, 1926 in Budapest, Hungary. Their witnesses were Zelma's husband, Sabetaj Papo, and Greta's mother, Roza Pressburger:

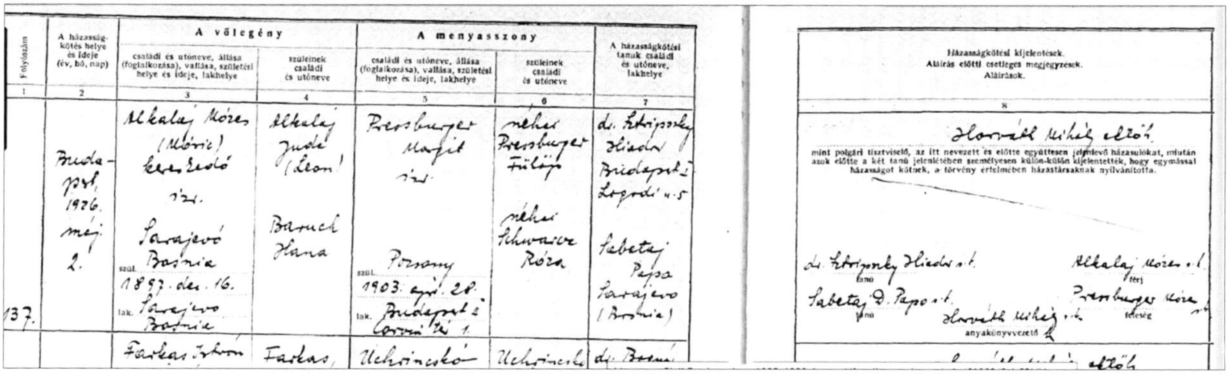

Folyószám	A házasságkötés helye és ideje (év, hó, nap)	A vőlegény: családi és utóneve, állása (foglalkozása), vallása, születési helye és ideje, lakhelye	A vőlegény: szüleinek családi és utóneve	A menyasszony: családi és utóneve, állása (foglalkozása), vallása, születési helye és ideje, lakhelye	A menyasszony: szüleinek családi és utóneve	A házasságkötési tanuk családi és utóneve, lakhelye
1	2	3	4	5	6	7
137.	Budapest, 1926. máj. 2.	Alkalaj Mózes (Móric) kereskedő izr. Sarajevó Bosnia szül. 1897. dec. 16. lak. Sarajevo Bosnia	Alkalaj Juda (Leon) Baruch Hana	Pressburger Margit izr. Pozsony szül. 1903. ápr. 28. lak. Budapest Corvin tér 1.	néhai Pressburger Fülöp néhai Schwarcz Róza	Sabetaj Papo Sarajevo (Bosnia)

Házasságkötési kijelentések.
Aláírás előtti esetleges megjegyzések.
Aláírások.

8

mint polgári tisztviselő, az itt nevezett és előtte együttesen jelenlevő házasulókat, miután azok előtte a két tanú jelenlétében személyesen külön-külön kijelentették, hogy egymással házasságot kötnek, a törvény értelmében házastársaknak nyilvánította.

Sabetaj D. Papo s. k. (tanú) — Alkalaj Mózes s. k. (férj) — Pressburger Margit s. k. (feleség)

anyakönyvvezető

Buki and Greta's marriage document, May 2, 1926

This document states Alkalaj, Mozes, born Sarajevo Bosnia 1897, dec 16, parents: Juda Leon Alkalaj and Hana Baruch married Pressburger, Margit, born Pozsony 1903, April 28, parents: Fulipo Pressburger and Roza Schwarz.

Greta and Buki were a mixed Jewish couple. That is, Greta was of Ashkenazim heritage (German or Eastern European) and Buki was of Sephardim heritage (Spain, Middle East). It wasn't common for the two heritages to intermarry. In the Appendix of the book, *The Jews of Yugoslavia*, by Harriet

Pass Freidenreich, Table 14 shows the percentage of intermarriages in ten-year spans tabulated from the registries of Jewish communities in Sarajevo. In 1926, the year Greta and Buki married, only 8.4% of the couples were mixed couples, Sephardim and Ashkenazim. If this had an impact on their relationship, we don't know. As my mother points out, "They were not together long enough as a family to note any issues."

Buki

Buki and Greta settled in Zagreb, Yugoslavia. Greta in those years was sporty and enjoyed cultural activities. She wanted to be a dancer and singer, but her father wouldn't let her pursue that path. Buki was a free spirit, riding his motorcycle and going for drinks after work. They were married for nine years before Greta, at the age of 32, gave birth to my mother.

Before Buki met Greta, he was an art student in Paris. When his father died of illness he returned home to help support his mother and the family. He became a furrier, as did his brother, Silvio. It is believed he owned three shops located in Belgrade, Sarajevo, and Zagreb. After their marriage, Greta worked for Buki. She helped customers to choose patterns and to choose an appropriate fur. Everything was made at the shops, which included such items as coats, jackets, hats, and muffs. Their furs were sold around the world. It so happens, Buki had a contact in NYC to whom he sent furs before his attempted escape from Yugoslavia. After the war, this contact found Greta in Israel and informed her that he still had furs from Buki. When my parents bought their first house, the sale of these furs helped them make the down payment.

Greta

I wondered how Buki became interested in the fur business. Historically, furs kept people warm in cold climates from the Balkans to Siberia, but were also used to show off status and to pay your taxes. For example, in Russia, until 1739, taxes could be paid with fox, beaver, sable and kuny furs. In Croatia, the national currency is called, "KUNA." Kuna is a type of marten known for its fur and used for currency as far back as medieval times.

While, it doesn't shed light on how Buki got involved with the fur business, we do know many Jewish families were involved with sewing. Perhaps Buki's interest in art and his time in France led to some interesting designs.

In 1935, my mother was born and given the name, Djurdjica/Judit (pronounced /jurjitza/). Though she was always called Djurdjica by her mother, my mom's name changed as she moved from one country to another country. My head spins a bit as my mom describes the name changes as follows:

> *Djurdjica is the Croatian spelling,[1] sometimes with "Dj" and sometimes just the "D" with a line through it to represent the sound as in "jury." "Jurjica" is the diminutive of "Jurja" which sounds in English a little like "Georgia." This is how I came to name my Guinea pig, "Georgina," a diminutive of Georgia. Leaving Sarajevo, I was "Gula" (the J, as in Julie"), on Korčula, I was "Giorgina," in Italy I was Guilia. Then in Israel, I used the Hebrew version of "Judit,""Jhudit" ("Judith" in English.) My friends and teachers called me, "Judith" And, before my trip, at the age of 17, from Israel to England, I obtained a passport and officially changed my name to Nirelle, a Hebrew name, in place of Djurdjica. Thus, I am known as Nirelle Judith Galson, née Alkalaj.*

Greta and Djurdjica[2]

1 In Yugoslavia, spoken languages were similar, with some variations. Serbs, Croats, Bosnians, Slovenes and Montenegrins lived there. Croatians, Bosnians, and Slovenes use the Latin alphabets. Serbs and Montenegrins use the Cyrillic alphabet. The Serbo-Croatian language uses both alphabets. More on this topic in the Notes section.

2 See Photo Gallery for photo of Djurdjica's birth certificate

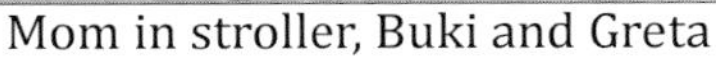

Mom in stroller, Buki and Greta

Greta and Mom

My mother's early years in Zagreb were ones of comfort and family, as one can imagine from surviving photos.

The lower left photo is Greta, dressed in one of Buki's furs, with Greta's sister Zelma and her husband, Sabataj on skis, holding my mother. The photo on the right is a cousin of my mother, Leonida, with my mother standing behind her. Both dressed in Buki's furs. My mother has fond memories of playing with Leonida. This comfortable time would end as WWII enveloped them, disrupting their lives, stealing their possessions, and taking family members, including Sabataj and Leonida.

Greta, Zelma, Djurdjica (my mom), Sabataj

Leonida and Djurdjica, (4-11-1940)

Buki's Fur Business

Buki in his automobile

Digging deep into the Internet, for any information about Buki's stores, I came across a few mentions of his business. One article by Lovorka Magaš, "Reklamni zavod Imago I komercijalni grafički dizajn u Hrvatskoj 1920-ih, (9-10-2008), "Advertising Images and Commercial Graphic Design Croatia in the 1920's," mentions that design work by Vladimir Mirosavljevic was done "between 1928 and 1930 for the fur shop Buki Alkalaj." Magaš's article includes these interesting graphics about another fur shop on Ilica Street in Zagreb. Buki's competition!

Ad for Krzna Vinicky, a competitor fur store

In the November 3, 1929 newspaper issue of "SLOVENEC" in its classified section, Buki placed an advertisement looking for a "Krznarske pomočnike" or "Fur assistant, seeking high pay for immediate opening."

Krznarske pomočnike
proti visoki plači za ta-
kojšnji nastop išče Buki
Alkalaj, Zagreb, Ilica 53 a

Buki's classified

One seeming discrepancy for the address in Zagreb is a telephone book page, which lists Buki at Ilica 55. Either he moved the store or expanded perhaps, we aren't quite sure.

In another article, this one by Melita Švob, "Sefardska židovska općina u Zagreb I Holokaust" or "Sephardic Jewish Community in Zagreb and the Holocaust" there is this example of a store advertisement by a Sephardic Jew, which coincidentally happens to be Buki's store (see photo to right).

This advertisement confirms Buki had a store in two cities. In Zagreb at 53 Ilica and in Sarajevo at Kralja Petra Ul. 6 (King Petra Street).

As of this writing, this is the only document I have found that mentions another store of Buki's outside Zagreb. My mother believes Buki had a store in Belgrade, but that has not yet been confirmed or identified.

Buki's store in Sarajevo was located on Kralja Petra Ul 6. The street name, Kralja Petra, or King Peter, has some history. According to the website, Destination Sarajevo, Kralja Petra Ul had various name changes as ruling parties changed. During Austro-Hungarian rule, this section of the street was named after Czar Franz Joseph. During the time of the Kingdom of Yugoslavia it was called Kralja Petra Street, which is where Buki's store was located. King Peter was King of Serbia and then King of Serbs, Croats and Slovenes until 1921. Then, during WWII, when Sarajevo was under the jurisdiction of the Independent State of Croatia (NDH) the name changed to Ulica Broj 1 (Street Number 1) and then again, after the war, in 1946, it became Jugoslovenske Narodne Armije (of the Yugoslav People's Army). Finally, in 1993, this section of the street became Zelenih Beretki (Green Berets, a volunteer army defending Sarajevo in 1991). I think Buki would be pleased to know that today Number 6 Zelenih Beretki houses a progressive art and design school for children.

A final mention of Buki's store appears in an article written by Vlasta Kovać, "Sephardi from Vlaska Street," in which he describes Jewish family businesses recorded in the Croatian State Archives. The entries are from June and July 1941 by the new Independent State of Croatia. Kovać notes that prior to WWII many Sephardic Bosnian Jews settled in Zagreb. Many of them were merchants who had shoe shops, leather processing, and fur shops. For example:

> *"Thus Josip Paps, born in Fojnica in 1909, owned a shoe store "Paps Shoes" in Jurisiceva 9, Salamon Pinto owned a larger shoe store in Ilica 35,* **Buki Alkalaj (Sarajevo 1897) also owned a fur trade in Ilica**, *while his surname and possibly cousin David Alkalaj (Brcko, 1891), son of Asher, owned an Alkalaj and Meyer skin and tannin factory in Heinzel 69 during the interwar period."*

Finding these mentions of Buki and his store, brings him to life. His story is that of a working man, a merchant, a designer, and a businessman growing his business.

Cousin Ellie (Zelma's daughter), Buki, and Greta

Family Lineage

These days there is great interest in tracing family roots as far back as possible. With immigration on the minds of most Americans, a common question is "From where does your family originate?" Usually, a person knows where their parents were born, maybe grandparents, and sometimes great grandparents, but beyond that can be more difficult to find answers. People are also curious about whether they look like their past relatives, have similar interests, or celebrate the same holidays in the same manner. For Jewish families, tracing family roots can be difficult. Forced immigrations, genocides and destructions of temples, means finding records can be impossible. Additionally, there were name changes along the way. In our case, "Alkalaj" even amongst family members is spelled or misspelled differently. "Alkalaj" is also "Alkalai," "Alkalay," "Alcalay" and in Hebrew "Alqala'y" or "Alqala'iy." The Spanish version is "Alcalá," which comes from the Arabic word "alqal'ah" meaning "the fort" or "the citadel." One internet site notes that "Alkalai" is the Hebrew version among Sephardic Jews that came from Spain. Jewish last names often took the name of the place where they were living. Alkalaj is directly related to the Spanish cities which use the name "Alcalá." The Jews were expelled from Spain in 1492.

To verify my mother's lineage, I looked at genealogical websites. Entering different spellings yielded sometimes confusing information, sometimes interesting information, and sometimes verified or cross-referenced pertinent information about our family. For example, Buki's brother is "Silvio" but, entering "Sylvio" brought up information about his football (soccer) playing days. However, before these tools were available, my mother found out about her lineage through family stories about ancestors. Verifying these stories is a challenge.

One such story from my grandmother Greta begins with, "One of your relatives was a famous Rabbi." June Engel, in her writeup about the Pressburger siblings, describes under Greta's name, her husband Buki's grandfather as a "famous Rabbi." This was corroborated in an interesting way. My mother worked for the Division of International Programs Abroad at Syracuse University for over 28 years. She served as associate director, director and then became its first Executive Director from 1993 to 2007. As part of her job, she would visit the programs in Italy, England, France, Holland, Spain, China, Zimbabwe, and Israel. Usually, she met with various staff members of Syracuse University or of the local institutions with whom she might be coordinating. There would be the usual office meetings, on-site tours, perhaps a local tour, and casual dinners.

However, in Israel, my mother had a very unusual change from the expected meetings:

> *A special reception was arranged with the president of the university with a beautiful presentation of food and a small crowd of people. I had never met with the president of any university while traveling abroad. What was this all about? I wondered. When I inquired, I was told 'Don't you know? You are famous!'*

They explained that, her great grandfather (Buki's grandfather) was a famous Rabbi to the Israelis. It turns out that, Rabbi Judah ben Solomon Chai Alkalai (1798-1878) was an early influence on what would become the Zionist movement (or the belief in the establishment of a Jewish State and the return of the Jewish people to the Land of Israel).

Rabbi Alkalai was born in Sarajevo, Bosnia which at the time, was ruled by the Ottoman Empire. He was Sephardic, meaning he could trace his heritage back to Spain, which was why he spoke the Ladino language. He studied in Jerusalem which was also under the Ottoman Empire. He then moved to Semlin, Belgrade, which was under the Austrian Empire, where he taught and became a Rabbi. He wrote influential essays and books. In 1857, he wrote "Return of the Jews to the Holy Land and renewed glory of Jerusalem." Another leader of the Zionist movement, Theodor Herzl was influenced by Alkalai. Herzl's grandfather attended the synagogue where Judah Alkalai was the Rabbi. Certainly, their friendship included many discussions on the topic of the Jewish people returning to the land of Israel. Rabbi Alkalai traveled around Europe discussing his ideas on the Jewish peoples return to the Holy Land. One idea he had was to raise money to buy land from the Ottoman Empire. It is as if he knew already that trouble was ahead for the Jewish people because he talked about the need to accomplish this before 1940, at which time it would become much more difficult for the Jewish people. Was he predicting WWII? A few years before his death, he moved to Jerusalem and established a Jewish colony. Rabbi Alkalai is buried in the Mount of Olives Jewish Cemetery in Israel.

Ester and Judah Alkalai

It could also be that this famous Rabbi Alkalai, with the same last name as my grandfather Buki, is a red herring. Maybe it is through the lineage of Buki's mother, whose maiden name is "Baruh" also spelled, Baruch. In Sarajevo, there is a cemetery, founded in 1630, with a tombstone for the first rabbi of Sarajevo, Samuel Baruch (Baruh), perhaps he is also the "famous Rabbi" in the family stories.

Another story begins, "After the expulsion from Spain, one of your relatives worked for a vizier of the Ottoman Empire!" Here is a map of the Ottoman Empire. If our family indeed came from Spain, how did we get to Bosnia? Maybe through Egypt and up the coast, or maybe through Greece (Morea) or Italy.

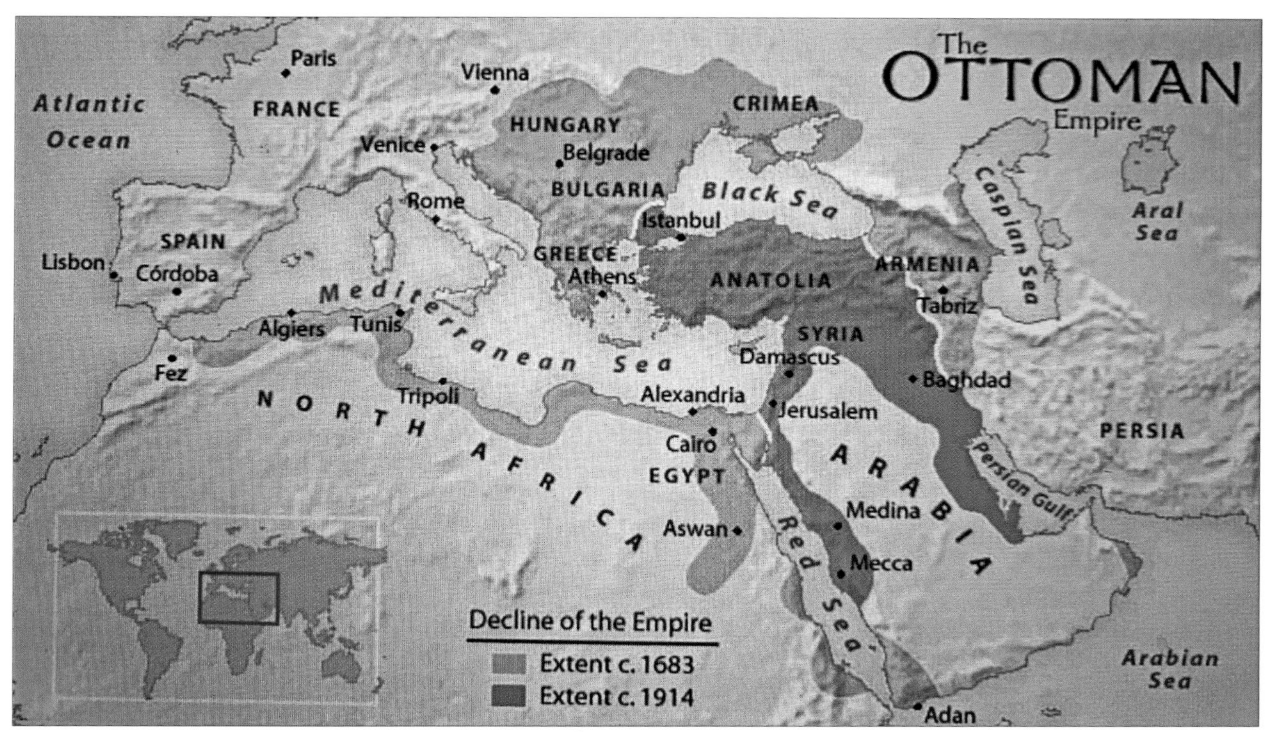

Map of Ottoman Empire

While retracing my mother's journey, my husband Paul and I visited Dubrovnik, an ancient port city of Croatia. The archivist of Dubrovnik mentioned that many Jewish families living in Sarajevo emigrated there through the port in Dubrovnik. He had a list of names of Jews who came to Dubrovnik. Alkalaj and Papo were listed, but there was no way to verify family connections. By the way, the synagogue in Dubrovnik is the oldest Sephardic synagogue still in use today and the second oldest synagogue in Europe.

There is a list of all the viziers of the Ottoman Empire and one can see quite a few were of Bosnian origin, especially from 1497-1650. So perhaps this family member was inspired by the vizier to live in what is now Bosnian territory and where our more recent relatives were born. Or, perhaps, we were already settled in the Bosnian area and a relative got a job with the Bosnian vizier ruling within the Ottoman Empire of that time period. Why would this story be passed down, if it wasn't true?!

Abridged History of Yugoslavia

On the cover of my mother's passport shown here, "Kraljevina Jugoslavija" Croatian for "Kingdom of Yugoslavia," and in the French, "Royaume de Yougoslavie." Passport is "Passeport" in French and "Putna Isprava" in Croatian. Today neither the "Kingdom" nor "Yugoslavia" exist. What happened? It's a long story which I will address towards the end of this history. For now, let's focus on the establishment of Yugoslavia.

Mom's Passport
Issued April 1938

Prior to WWI, the Austro-Hungarian Empire was composed of many different ethnic regions. After WWI the Empire was broken up into many independent regions. The new "Kingdom of the Serbs, Croats, and Slovenes," was proclaimed. This brought together the former south-Slav subjects of Austria and Hungary, with those of the former Kingdom of Serbia. Peter I was the first king until his death in 1921 and was succeeded by his son, Alexander I.

There was a lot of tension between the different groups in this new democracy, primarily between the Catholic Croats and the Orthodox Serbs. By 1929, the tensions collapsed the democracy. In its place a Serb dominated dictatorship was established under Alexander I, and the country was renamed the Kingdom of Yugoslavia (meaning: land of Southern Slavs), hence the title on my mother's passport.

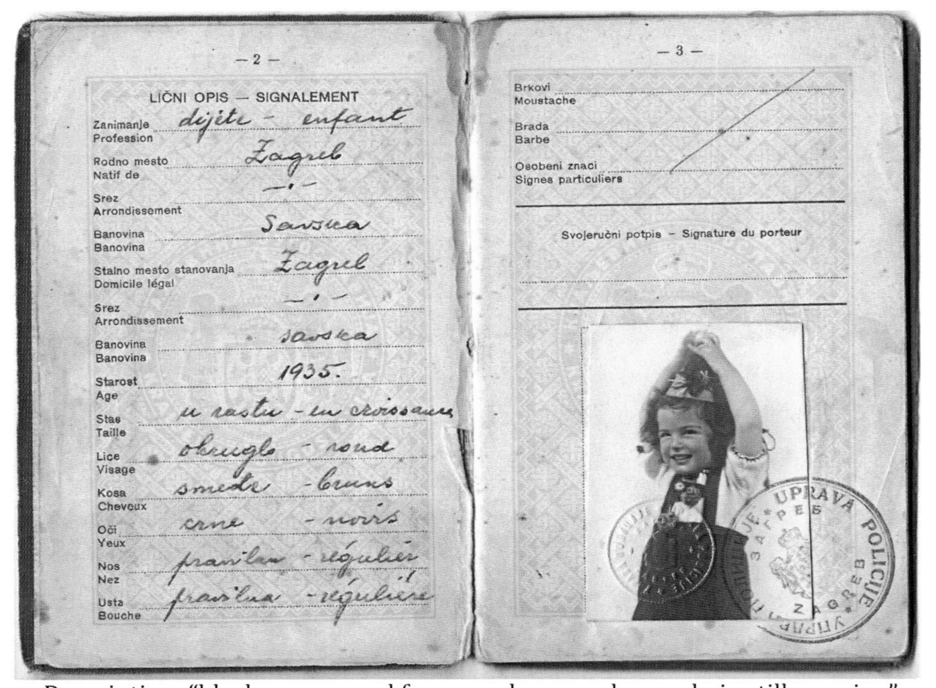
— 2 —

LIČNI OPIS — SIGNALEMENT

Zanimanje / Profession: dijete - enfant
Rodno mesto / Natif de: Zagreb
Srez / Arrondissement: -"-
Banovina / Banovina: Savska
Stalno mesto stanovanja / Domicile légal: Zagreb
Srez / Arrondissement: -"-
Banovina / Banovina: savska
Starost / Age: 1935.
Stas / Taille: u rastu - en croissance
Lice / Visage: okruglo - rond
Kosa / Cheveux: smeđe - bruns
Oči / Yeux: crne - noirs
Nos / Nez: pravilan - régulier
Usta / Bouche: pravilna - régulière

— 3 —

Brkovi / Moustache
Brada / Barbe
Osobeni znaci / Signes particuliers
Svojeručni potpis - Signature du porteur

UPRAVA POLICIJE ZAGREB

Description: "black eyes, round face, regular nose, brown hair, still growing"

Kingdom of Yugoslavia

In response, some Croats, led by Ante Pavelić, formed the fascist organization Ustashi to oppose the Serbs. In 1934 they managed to assassinate King Alexander I, though the dictatorship remained in control. The following year my mother was born in Zagreb, in the Kingdom of Yugoslavia.

From 1935-1939, seemingly all is well with Buki, family, and business. Yet big changes are just about to rock their lives. WWII began in September 1939, with Germany's invasion of Poland, and throughout 1940 Hitler rises in power. Meanwhile, the Ustashi in Yugoslavia aligned themselves with Hitler's racial theories in a desire for a racially pure Croatia. In less than one month, Yugoslavia had some dramatic developments, which immediately affected my mother's family.

- On March 25, 1941 the Yugoslav Prime Minister, Drags Cvetkovic, signed an alliance called the Tripartite Pact in Vienna, with the Axis powers: Germany (Adolf Hitler), Italy (Benito Mussolini), and Japan (Emperor Hirohito). [Cvetkovic did not have support at home for the alliance and two days later, Cvetkovic's government was overthrown by his military and General Simovic's new government renounces the agreement.]
- On April 6, 1941, just two weeks later, Germany invaded Yugoslavia, bombing Belgrade for three days and moving into Yugoslavia with troops.
- On April 17, 1941 Yugoslavia surrenders to Germany and Italy
- In April 1941 Germany and Italy re-established the Kingdom of Yugoslavia as a puppet state referred to as The Independent State of Croatia (NDH).

At this point, the Axis powers divided Yugoslavia into two administrative areas:

- The Ustashi were put in charge of the Independent State of Croatia (NDH).
- The Italians took over the central Dalmatian coast, including Split and Korčula, a long coveted area for Italy.

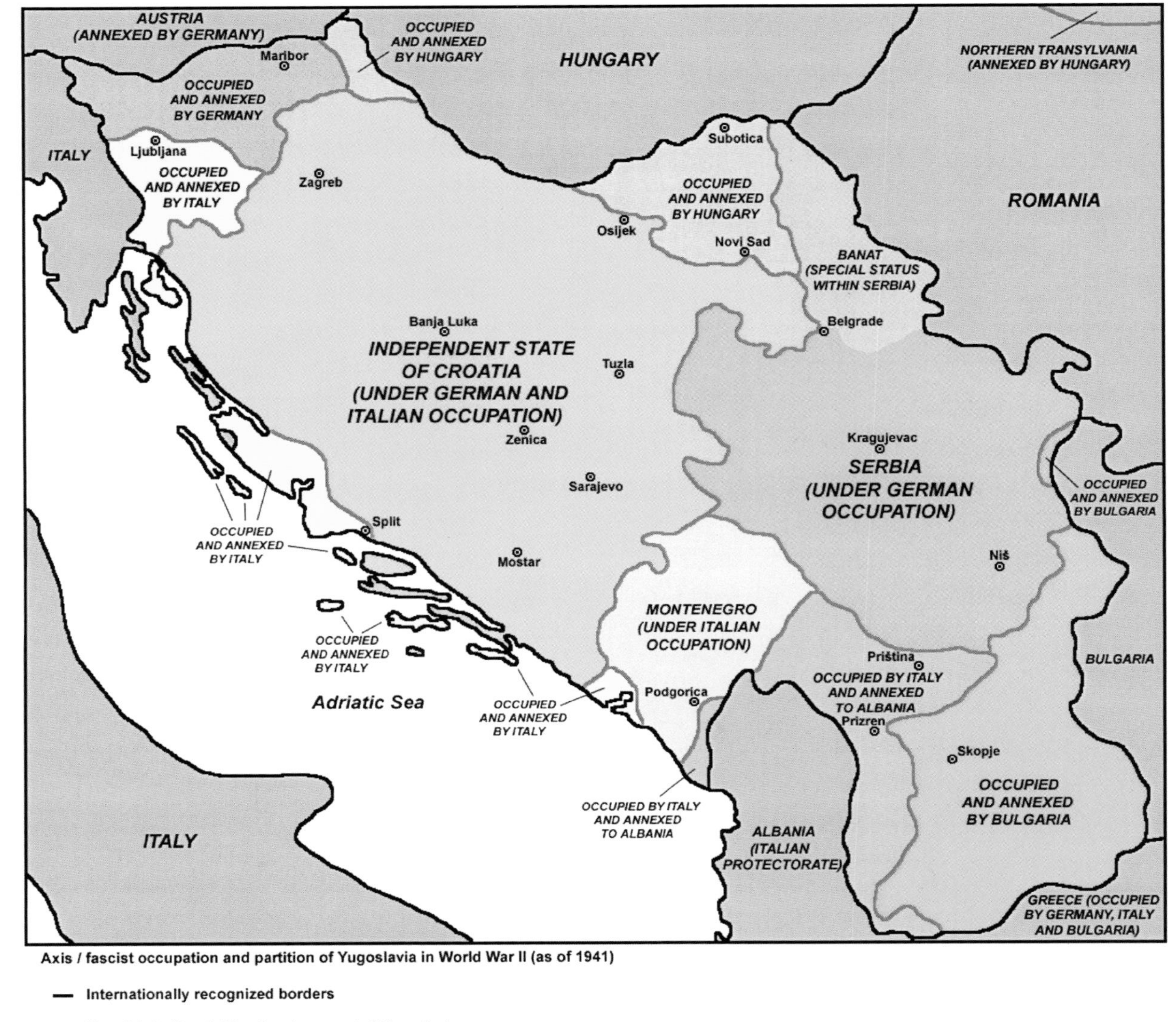

Axis / fascist occupation and partition of Yugoslavia in World War II (as of 1941)

- Internationally recognized borders
- Illegal Axis / fascist borders in occupied Yugoslavia
- Independent State of Croatia (German and Italian occupation)
- Serbia (German occupation)
- Banat, region with special status within Serbia (German occupation and local German administration)
- Montenegro (Italian occupation)
- Occupied and annexed by Bulgaria
- Occupied and annexed by Nazi Germany
- Occupied and annexed by Italy
- Occupied and annexed by Italy (As a part of Italian protectorate of Albania)
- Occupied and annexed by Hungary

Note: Some scholars are suggesting that term "fascist" is not a proper description for all countries that participated in occupation of Yugoslavia. Other scholars (including those from former Yugoslavia) are using this term as a description for all these countries.

Map of Partition of Yugoslavia in WWII, 1941

https://commons.wikimedia.org/wiki/Atlas_of_Yugoslavia#/media/File:Axis_occupation_of_Yugoslavia,_1941-43.png

As a result, a resistance movement known as the "Partisans" formed to fight both the Ustashi and the Nazi occupation. The Partisans were a communist backed organization led by Josip Tito, who later became the head of Yugoslavia after the war (and was commonly known as Marshal Tito).

Adolf Hitler shaking hands with Ante Pavelić

By the end of April 1941, the Ustashi began a brutal suppression of Serbs, Jews, and Roma (gypsies). They passed race laws protecting the Aryan blood of the Croatian people, and began printing anti-Semitic propaganda. Jewish property had to be reported to the authorities. Soon after, concentration camps were established, and deportation began for Jews, Romas, Muslims and Serbs; the latter being the largest group.

As life for Jews worsened in Zagreb, Buki, a Serbian and a Jew, must have been anxious to leave Zagreb. Greta says in her interview, "everyone was anxious. We knew the Germans were near by." So, Buki, Greta, and Djurdjica drove from Zagreb to Belgrade, where Buki may have had a store or needed to attend to some business.

Reflecting back to when she was five years old, my mother remembers this frightening drive:

It was an extremely scary ride. You could hear bombs. I knew we were escaping from danger.

And, then they moved from Belgrade to Sarajevo. As Greta explains,

Buki said, you take the child and go to your sister in Sarajevo. It was less dangerous inside of the country than in other parts. I left with Nirelle by train. There were millions of people escaping. The war hadn't started, but people were afraid. Buki stayed in Belgrade. I didn't know if he would make it safely to Sarajevo, but after three days he arrived. He had to hide along the way, bringing a rug to lie down on and some food. The war was already on.

Remember too, in Sarajevo, Buki had the additional store, where he no doubt needed to attend to business. It is also where Buki's mother, Hannah Alkalj and Greta's oldest sister, Zelma Papo resided.

SARAJEVO

SARAJEVO HAD A LARGE NON-CROATIAN COMMUNITY, which initially made it a safer place for Jews. However, the Ustashi rapidly extended their control into Sarajevo and Bosnia overall.

To help understand what the Jewish population experienced in Sarajevo under the Ustashi, I read an article by Francine Friedman, "Writing for Survival: Letters of Sarajevo Jews Before Their Liquidation During WWII." In it she describes life in Sarajevo between 1941 and 1942 through letters written by local Jews to officials, asking for assistance with the following rules that had been put in place by the Ustashi:

April 17 - Jewish citizenship and protection revoked
April 27 - Jews no longer allowed to visit public places
May 7 - Jews no longer allowed to own radios and telephones
May 11 - Jews ordered to register their savings, business sheets, stocks, etc.
May 18 - Jews forced to identify their stores

Friedman explains that Jewish stores were no longer permitted to be controlled by their owners and a "povjerenik" or commissioner was appointed to run the business and collect profits. The letters in the article, dated from June to September, ask for financial assistance with such things as rent, or for the povjerenik to be expelled for improper handling of the store. All requests were denied, of course.

The family stayed with Greta's sister, Zelma for two weeks. Greta continues her story:

We couldn't stay there very long. We slept and ate in the basement. There were others there. They came from the street, people escaping from the street. Sometimes I went to the 9th floor where Zelma stayed and brought some food down. Slowly, slowly we are thinking how we should escape. Buki said, we should leave the city and go to the country where the peasants live. Buki knew a man, working with the Partisans. Sometimes he disappeared to the mountains. He was a Jewish man, a doctor. They called him, Ćića, which means Uncle [in Serbian, meaning a familiar older man]. He gave us a house to live in as ordinary peasants. We went out of the town dressed as peasants.

Seeking safety, the family moves to a village named Zlatinje. My mother has a few memories of their stay at this farm in the countryside. One is gardening with her father. There wasn't a lot of food due to the war, so Buki tried to grow vegetables. The soil was wonderful, and she remembers potatoes as especially fun to harvest. This indicates they were there in August when potatoes are harvested. Years later, at the boarding school in Israel, she would think of her father and their time together in the garden. When it was suggested to start a garden behind the school, she was the only student interested. The garden in Israel became a bed of zinnias. Zinnias remain as special flowers to my mom.

One day, the Ustashi gathered up some peasants near where Buki, Greta, and my mom were living. Greta recalls:

Everybody knows they took away some peasants. They were not Catholics, they were Serbians. The Ustashi were against the Serbs. The last policemen walking behind the row of peasants looked at Nirelle and asked, 'What is that for a child? This is a child? This is not an ordinary child. Who are you? Are you a little Jew?' She lifted her shoulders, she shrugged because she didn't know.

My mother remembers this moment too:

They asked me whose child I was. I was scared and didn't respond. These men told my mother that I shouldn't be outside because I clearly didn't look like a village kid.

Then the men searched the farmhouse and found two packages of pearls and also took Buki away. The men returned two days later and demanded more valuables. Greta continues:

I told them I don't know if there is anything else. They found only a half napoleon dollar [a French gold coin] in a pocket. That's all they found because the rest we buried in the earth. I said, 'there you found what you were looking for'. Then, they said, 'tell me immediately everything about your husband or I kill you like a dog. I stood there calm with my child and said, 'I know what you can do. If you think you can do it, then I stay here. He was ashamed. He said, 'Tomorrow I shall bring your husband back. When you come to town, you must wear the Jewish star and I won't do anything to you'.

Buki returned the next day. He reported the Jews were being arrested and taken away. This was a sad and dreadful situation. Again, Greta continues:

We knew then this was a serious situation. Still, Buki did not want to leave. In the evening, there was a beautiful moon. We sat looking out and Buki said, 'This is a beautiful place'. I looked at the distance and saw everything on fire.

And so, the next morning they returned to Sarajevo. My mother wrote a vignette about her experience in Zlatinje. In this excerpt, my mother shares through Djurdica's voice how she felt about leaving:

When my father comes back my parents talk away from me. Then my father comes to me and hugs me. Two days later we go back to Sarajevo where my aunt Zelma lives. I don't know why. I liked Zlatinje, working in the garden with my father and milking the goat with my mother. In the car I ask why we are leaving. My mother says: "because we are Jewish and some people do not like us." Why, I ask her. She does not know and I am scared again; of people in uniform. I am almost six, but do not know why people do not like us.

And, Greta adds to the moment with these words:

Before we knew what they were doing to the Jews, I had given a coat to a friend to take care of. I sewed money into that coat. When we returned to Sarajevo we went to her home and learned that she was one of the first they took away.

Buki and Greta understood they had to leave Sarajevo as soon as possible. Imagine, you are six years old standing at a train station, the sun has set, it is dark. You are with a group of strangers trying to escape. You take nothing with you so as not to look like you are traveling out of the country. Just a money bag hidden under your clothes or sewn into various spaces in the clothes you have layered on yourselves. That's the scene for my mother.

Greta, my mother, Zelma, and her husband Sabetai Papo, along with a group of other Jews, were waiting to take a train out of Sarajevo. At the train station, Sabetai became ill. The group tried to give him coffee and see to his well-being but, when the train pulls in, Sabetai and Zelma did not get on with the rest of the group. However, only a few stops later, the police entered the train and took this group of Jews by train back to Sarajevo and placed them in a small jail where they were fingerprinted, and women and men were separated.

Fearful and exhausted, my mother laid down on the cold floor, and fell asleep listening to the women discussing who should sleep next to the toilet, a hole in the floor. In the morning, Greta told my mother she dreamt that all her teeth fell out, and that meant someone had died. Indeed, when Zelma heard they were caught and at the jail, she walked past their window wearing black, sending the message to the family that her husband, Sabetai, had died.

Inside the jail, my mother was allowed to leave the women's quarters to visit her father where the men were kept. So, the women pinned messages under her skirt to send to the men. Again, my mother knew to be careful not to let the guards know. Scary? Yes. Fortunately, after about one week in jail, her Aunt Zelma was able to bribe someone in order to have my mother released. Unfortunately, Zelma brought her to stay with a stranger, which was also scary for my mother. Greta also shared these stories about her time in the prison:

> *It was terrible. We were about 35 women. We exercised by dancing and doing other such things to keep up our spirits. We were let outside for five minutes every day. Zelma brought me a small pillow. One of the other women had a needle. I used this needle to pull out the threads stitch by stitch, then I folded money into tiny bits and put it into the feathers, then sewed it back up. One of the women was the wife of a rabbi. One of the officers at the prison had grown up visiting this rabbi's wife and remembered sitting on her lap. Several times someone came to speak with her. Then, they let us all out on Erev Yom Kippur. We were lucky. We could have ended up at a concentration camp.*

After a month at the prison, Greta felt it was unbelievable they were let out on Yom Kippur, which was October 1, 1941.

This photo is a government building that Paul and I were shown by an archivist in Sarajevo. It is across the street from the National Archive and a possible location where this group was held. We also saw photos, at the Jewish Museum of Sarajevo, of other locations where Jews were held.

Not long after this, the family again tried to escape from Sarajevo. This time, Buki paid a Turkish man to escort my mother and Greta, with them posed as wife and child. On their travel documents, their last names became that of the man's and their first names became Bhula and Jula (Greta and mom). They dressed as muslims with appropriate garments covering themselves, and the man wore a fez. Again, they boarded a train in Sarajevo and successfully fled to Mostar, where they stayed in an apartment until they could continue on to Split. At this point in the war, Split was controlled by the Italians and was a safe city for Jews.

Buki remained in Sarajevo for various reasons. He needed to attend to some business and certainly could not be seen with Bhula and Jula. Buki needed to obtain his own travel documents, which Greta was helping to aquire in Mostar. He planned to travel by the same train to meet Greta in Mostar. However, Buki and a friend of his were caught and taken by a different train to the Jasenovac Concentration Camp. This friend survived the War. Here is what Greta says about this friend who she met once in Palestine:

> *This friend told me that when they arrived at Jasenovac, they asked who was ill. Buki probably felt he might be safer at the hospital. So, he raised his hand. However, these individuals were lined up and each and every one of them shot. One day, this friend went on a work detail in the woods. His guards were killed by Partisans and he escaped. He fought with the Partisans then came to Palestine.*

And, so Buki's life was taken by the Ustashi in 1941 at the Jasenovac Concentration Camp. When I ask my mother, "Why did Buki stay behind?" Her answer is,

> *"I believe he stayed to take care of some business. He also felt safe in Sarajevo as that is where he was from. He was of the people. He belonged."*

In a city within a country with a divided ethnic confrontation of one people against another as part of your history, perhaps you get used to the angry noise and the outrages. Genocide was unimaginable, unthinkable in a civilized community. Why should he fear for his life in the very place he was born, where his family lived for years, where his Sephardic Jewish ancestors settled long ago under the safety of the Ottoman Empire?

Jasenovac Memorial

<u>Jasenovac</u>

Concentration camps and mass killing sites were located throughout Yugoslavia. Starting in May of 1941, the reign of terror began for Serbs, Jews and

Romas (the Roma are also referred to as Gypsies.) After visiting concentration camps in Germany, the Ustashe built a new complex of camps, within a 70 mile area, known as Jasenovac, with its main camp located near the village of Jasenovac. The area was chosen because it was near existing factories and the railway system. It was also swampy and bordered the rivers of Sava and Una, making it easy to hide its operations and difficult for prisoners to escape. Camps I and II operated from May to November 1941, at which time the detainees were moved to these new camps. Camps III, IV,[3] and V were the largest camps in operation until liberation at the end of the war. Camp III was the main camp located outside the village of Jasenovac and referred to as "Ciglana" (Brickyard). Camp IV was inside the village and named, "Kozara" (Tannery). Camp V went by the name, Stara Gradiska. Gypsies were brought to the village of Ustica and women and children to Jablanac; these were smaller "specialty" camps.

Train cars which carried victims to Jasenovac

The number of victims specifically at the Jasenovac sites is difficult to ascertain due to the destruction of evidence. It is estimated that the Ustashi murdered around 600,000 Serbs, Jews, and Romas.

The Jasenovac Memorial site is located at the edge of the Jasenovac village, about 60 miles south of Zagreb. Although hundreds of thousands were killed here, the memorial lists only the individual names of known victims at the Jasenovac camps totaling 83,145, which includes: 13,116 Jews, 16,173 Roma (Gypsies), 47,627 Serbs, 4,255 Croats, and 1,128 Bosnian Muslims.

Jews living in Croatia were also sent to concentration camps in other parts of Yugoslavia and to Auschwitz in Germany. Of the 40,000 Jews living in Croatia before the war, only 9,000 survived.

Over 300,000 Serbs were killed, and another 300,000 were deported to Serbia. Twenty-five thousand Roma, virtually all of the population in Croatia, were killed.

Inside the Museum at the Jasenovac Memorial site, victim's names are etched or printed onto panels hanging

3 In the Palestine section, I write more on camp IV, where Buki's brother, Silvio was sent.

from the ceiling and hung on walls. Paul and I found Buki's name and several family members on the wall panel at the end of this hall.

Buki Alkalaj

Leonida Alkalaj (wife of Silvio)

Silvio Alkalaj (Buki's brother)

And, here is how Buki is listed in the online *Holocaust Survivors and Victims Database:*

BUKI ALKALAJ
Sex: Male
Father Name: LEON
Date of Birth: 1897* [1897]
Place of Birth: SARAJEVO, SARAJEVO
Nationality/Ethnicity: ŽIDOV [Jewish]
Cause of Death: Killed (UBIJEN)
Killed: By the Ustasha (OD USTAŠA)
Year of Death: 1942* [1942]
Death Place: In camp (U LOGORU)
Camp: JASENOVAC

The Jewish Museum of Sarajevo has stories of Jews escaping during WWII, and of the "Righteous" who helped them. It was riveting to read that a few were similar to my mother's experience. Francine Friedman (see prior mention), and also the archivists we spoke to in Split, explained that mostly wealthy people, who could pay their way out, were able to escape.

To help the persecuted, the Righteous were also risking their lives. On the wall at the Jewish Museum of Sarajevo there are stories of some of the Righteous. For example, one story describes how when the Germans entered the region, Marko Božić, from the Resistance Movement, helped Josef Sinković-Singer, his wife, and their daughter to move from the city to a village where they could hide. In another, Ratio Janković accompanied a Jewish woman dressed as a Muslim on the train until they were safely to the Italian occupied zone. And, Sadik Ahmed Saralop, a salesman who traded with merchants in Sarajevo and other cities, helped a family get to the Italian safe zone. Saralop's story ends with, "After being informed on, he was deported to Jasenovac where he was killed for rescuing Jews."

After reading that last sentence of Saralop's story and seeing the photo of this man wearing a fez, I had to wonder, did this man help Buki? Did the man who helped Buki get caught? On the other hand, one family rumor says, "perhaps the Turkish man who helped Buki, turned Buki in and that is how Buki was caught." But, maybe this family story isn't quite accurate. Hopefully our Turkish man was one of the Righteous too.

SADIK AHMED SARALOP • Sarajevo

Ahmed Sadik Saralop, otac Zeinebe Hardage, Pravednika među narodima, rođen je u Grčkoj u Solunu (Saloniki). Iz Soluna je preselio u Makedoniju (Bitola), gdje je trgovao s mnogim Jevrejima. Naučio je i ladino jezik. Najprijatnije se osjećao u jevrejskom kvartu u Bitoli. Godine 1931. Ahmed je stigao u Sarajevo, a najviše je trgovao s Isidorom Papom. I postali su dobri prijatelji. Nakon izvjesnog vremena, otišao je u Konjic, gdje je otvorio trgovinu. Imao je običaj sjediti u kafani na željezničkoj stanici, pijuckajući kafu i razmatrajući vijesti u svijetu, tako da je bio dobro upućen o užasima u Sarajevu i sudbini Jevreja. Jednog dana, sredinom 1941. godine, dok je sjedio u toj kafani, vidio je svog prijatelja Isidora Papu, koji je stigao iz Dubrovnika sa suprugom i dvoje djece kako ulaze u voz za Sarajevo. Ahmed je skočio i požurio prema prijatelju, pitajući ga s čuđenjem: "Gdje ideš, Isidore?" Zgrabio je Papine kofere i djecu i izvukao ih iz voza. Bez oklijevanja, Ahmed ih je odmah odveo svojoj kući, gdje su ostali dok su sredili potrebne dokumente koji bi im omogućili da dođu do zone pod italijanskom okupacijom. Za svoja herojska djela za vrijeme rata Ahmed Sadik Saralop je platio životom. Neko je izdao Ahmeda jer je pomagao Jevrejima. Ahmed je deportovan u Jasenovac, gdje je mučki ubijen.

Ahmed Sadiq-Saralop, the father of Zayneba Hardaga, Righteous Among the Nations, was born in Salonika, Greece. From there, he moved to Monastir (Bitola), where he traded with many Jews and even learned to speak Ladino. He felt most at home in the Jewish quarter of Bitojla. In 1913, Sadiq-Saralop arrived in Sarajevo, where he traded mostly with Isidor Papo, a thread merchant. They became good friends. After a while, Sadiq-Saralop moved to Konjic, where he opened a shop. Sadiq-Saralop had the custom of sitting at a cafe in the railway station, sipping coffee slowly and catching up on the world news. Thus, he was well informed about the horrors transpiring in Sarajevo and the destiny of the Jews. One day in mid-1941, while sitting in the cafe, he saw his friend Isidor Papo arrive from Dubrovnik with his wife and two children and change on to a train heading for Sarajevo. Sadiq-Saralop leapt up, rushed towards his friend, and asked in astonishment: "Where are you going Isidor?" He grabbed the Papos' suitcases and Isidor's children and pulled them off the train. Without hesitating, Sadiq-Saralop took them directly to his home, where they stayed until arrangements could be made for them to acquire documents that would enable them to reach the Italian occupied zone. For his heroic wartime deeds, Ahmed Sadiq-Saralop paid with his life. After being informed on, he was deported to Jasenovac on the last transport where he was killed for rescuing Jews.

Photo of one of the stories of the Righteous on the wall of the Jewish Museum of Sarajevo.

MOSTAR

City of Mostar The bridge in the photo is the Stari Bridge crossing the Neretva River. It was originally built during the Ottoman Empire and survived 427 years before being destroyed during the Croatian - Bosnian War 1992-1994 and then rebuilt.

In Mostar, Greta and my mom stayed in an apartment for some time because Greta was trying to get the travel document (also referred to as a Laissez-Passer) which Buki needed for safe passage to meet them in Mostar. From my interview with Greta, she explains:

> *I had a small photo of Buki. It was very expensive to get the passage. I gave this man a lot of jewelry. It was arranged that he would meet Buki in Sarajevo. He left at night and arrived in the early morning at 6am. He was supposed to meet Buki at 7am. But, he found out he was already taken. I was waiting at night for the train. When it arrived I saw only the man walking towards me and then he told me Buki was taken by the police.*

And, the only memory my mother has of Mostar is that:

> *My mother would sometimes go out dressed as a Muslim and carried a knife behind her back because it was not safe to be a woman walking alone and figured she would draw less attention to herself. She also carried money sewn into her clothing.*

Again, this young child was aware that her mother was doing something dangerous and it was scary.

Why was Greta protecting herself as a Muslim in Mostar? Mostar was under Italian rule, but not necessarily a safe place to live. In the division of control, there were more Croats living in the Independent State of Croatia, NDH, controlled by the Ustashi, and more Serbs and Muslims living in the area controlled by the Italians, including Mostar and Split. In June 1941, a large number of Serbs were arrested, shot, and thrown into the Neretva River. The Serbs were in slightly more danger than the Jews. Muslims were divided, some supporting the Ustashi against the Serbs and some supporting the Partisans against the Ustashi. In Mostar, Muslims were supporting the Partisans. Greta perhaps had a sense that she wasn't safe as a Jew, an Ashkenazi Hungarian Jew (Hungary supported Hitler and his invasion of Yugoslavia), married to a Sephardic Jew. The faster she headed to Split, the better.

SPLIT

Split/Spljet (Croatian), Spalato (Italian)

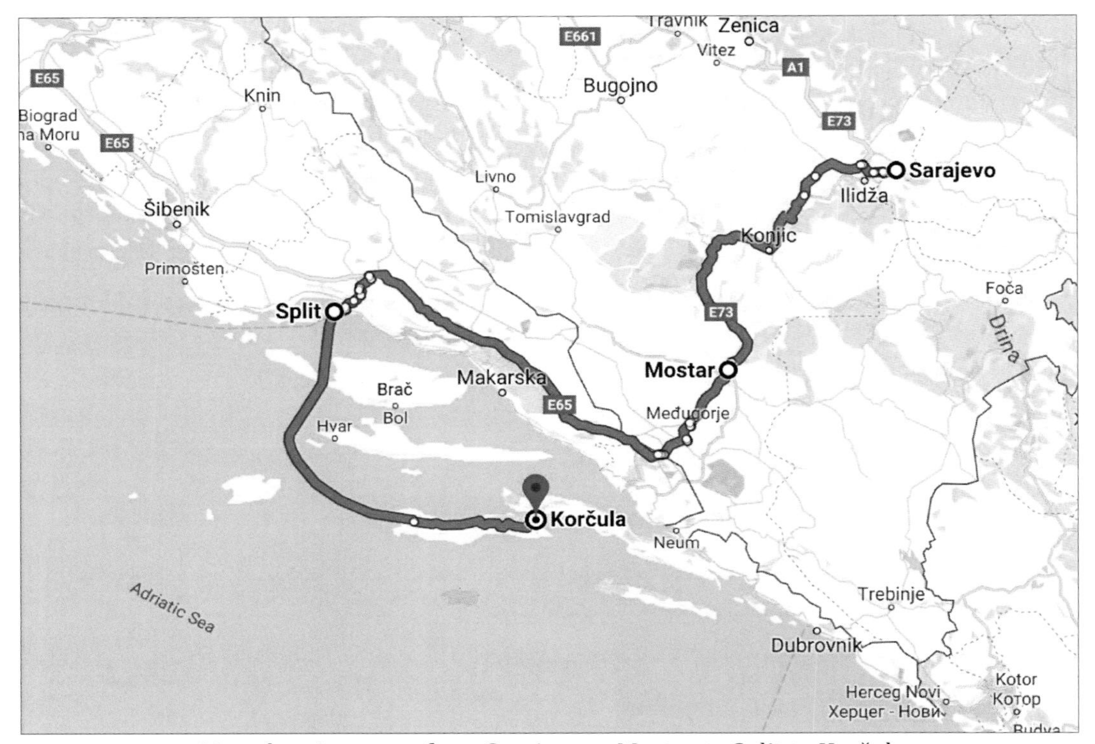

Map showing route from Sarajevo to Mostar to Split to Korčula

When Greta and my mom arrived in Split from Mostar, they spent just a short time there, so my mother has only a few memories of the city. One memorable event occurred along the promenade at the city waterfront.

> *The boats were tied to the promenade which had about a four foot high wall. I remember fishing along this wall and falling in. There were no ladders to swim to, so people had to reach down to pull me out!*

When Paul and I visited Split, we saw a gentleman slip into the water from a "submarine" tourist boat. Because the boat had curved sides and no ladder, he could not get up the side of the boat. He was

a large man and the people on the promenade had trouble lifting him out. He had to swim past several boats until he found a boat with a ladder, where he too was pulled out by several men!

Split, the second largest city in Croatia, is a beautiful city on the coast of the Adriatic Sea. The Roman emperor Diocletian built a palace at this location and the city expanded beyond its' walls. There was a small Jewish presence inside the palace from the earliest days. Located inside the palace is the third oldest European synagogue, which is still in use. It was built in the16th Century on the second floor of a medieval house.

The left photo below, is a corridor inside Diocletian's palace. The sign on the left wall of this corridor (a street) reads, "Entrance into the one-time Jewish Ghetto."

Photo on left: Entrance to Jewish Ghetto on Židovski Prolaz. Down the street in the distance, Paul stands at the stairwell to the Synagogue, which also serves today as the Jewish Community Center. Photo on right: Gate to the Synagogue, closed the day we visited.

Beginning in 1420 when the Venetians gained control of Split, the Jews were fairly well protected until the 1700's when their rights began to be restricted. Many Jewish families left for Italy during the early 1800's. When Split became part of Austria the Jewish restrictions were lifted. By WWII only about four hundred Jews were living in Split.

In 1941, after the invasion of Yugoslavia by Germany, Italy, and Hungary and the country of divvied up, Split was placed under Italian control. The Italians did not allow the Ustashi to persecute the Jews during 1941. However, the Germans and the Ustashi were relentless in their pressure on the Italians to transfer the Jews to German officials. Then, in June 1942 the synagogue in Split was destroyed by a mob and Jewish businesses destroyed. At this point, the Italians decided to move the Jewish people and Jewish refugees living in Split to Italian camps on the Dalmatian Islands, where they would be safer.

In doing so, Greta, my mother, and a few thousand Jews living in the Italian occupied region of the newly established Independent State of Croatia were saved by the local Italian leadership.

At the United States Holocaust Memorial Museum, there is an interview of a survivor, Flory Jagoda, who traveled a similar route as my mother and grandmother, from Zagreb to Split to Korćula to Bari. Jagoda was a teenager at the time. She talks about the daily new restrictions on the Jews in Zagreb, from being told to go home from her school classroom to turning in their radios. She understood that the Jews were not safe, but not aware of concentration camps. Flory shares that when the family escaped to Split, they were still afraid the Italians would turn the Jews over to the Ustashi or the Germans. Then, she continues, three hundred Jews including herself were sent to Korćula. Perhaps, Greta and my mom were with her. At the time of the interview Flory was in her 80's and reflects on her admiration for the Italians and the people of Korćula who welcomed the refugees into their homes.

In late August 1942, Mussolini signed an order to give the Jewish refugees in the Italian controlled areas of Croatia over to the Germans. However, the Italian Foreign Ministry and the Italian military leadership in the zones of occupation along the Dalmatian coast were aware that the German intent was to transfer the Jews to concentration camps, where their fate was certainly death. For many months, the Foreign Ministry used administrative tactics to delay a transfer. The various communications are detailed and discussed in a lecture by Daniel Carpi, "The Rescue of Jews in the Italian Zone of Occupied Croats," preserved at the Shoah Resource Center at Yad Vashem, the Holocaust memorial in Israel.

There was some debate between the Italians about what to do with the Jews. The Interior Ministry in Italy did not want the Jews transferred to Italy. However, the Foreign Ministry of Italy was concerned that the Jews were living in too wide an area to protect them from local citizens who might report them to the Ustashi and the Germans. So, one option to better protect the Jews was to move them over to the Dalmatian Islands (Dalmatia is the coastal area of Croatia).

Of course, this begs the question, why did the Italians protect the Jews? Noted Holocaust researcher Jonathan Steinberg theorizes there was, "a kind of national conspiracy [among the Italian military] to frustrate the much greater and more systematic brutality of the Nazi state."

In Italy, the issue of race did not factor in until 1938 when Benito Mussolini enacted laws segregating the Jews and limiting their access to education and jobs. In 1940, the Italians opened

50 concentration camps, mostly for political prisoners and about 2000 foreign Jews. Italian Jews were not deported or sent to concentration camps [Moreover, the Italians were known to protect the Jewish populations in Greece, France and Yugoslavia as well.] In July of 1943, when Mussolini was overthrown, the concentration camps in Italy were slowly deactivated, yet in September 1943, when the Germans took over the northern and central part of Italy the Germans quickly began rounding up the Italian Jews, easily found due to the registrations Mussolini had put in place in 1938. Some 8,000 Italian Jews died at various concentration camps.

KORČULA

Korčula (Croatian) Curzola (Italian)

THE TIMING IS NOT CLEAR, but Greta and my mom, along with many other Jews in Split, were sent by ferry on a 3-hour boat ride to the island of Korčula (pronounced Korchula). Here, they registered with the local Italian authorities. They were able to live in an apartment in Korčula Old Town, at the southern end of the island. For Greta and my mom it was their home for one school year.

Greta's friend Bimba Beck[4] ran a small school for Jewish children on the island. However, Greta felt it safer to send my mom to the monastery where there was a school run by Catholic nuns. At this school, my mother's name is registered as Giorgina Alkalaj.

Bimba Beck

4 See Bimba Beck Interview describing her experience from Belgrade to Sarajevo to Korćula to Bari to the US: https://kentuckyoralhistory.org/ark:/16417/xt7dv40jwq9t

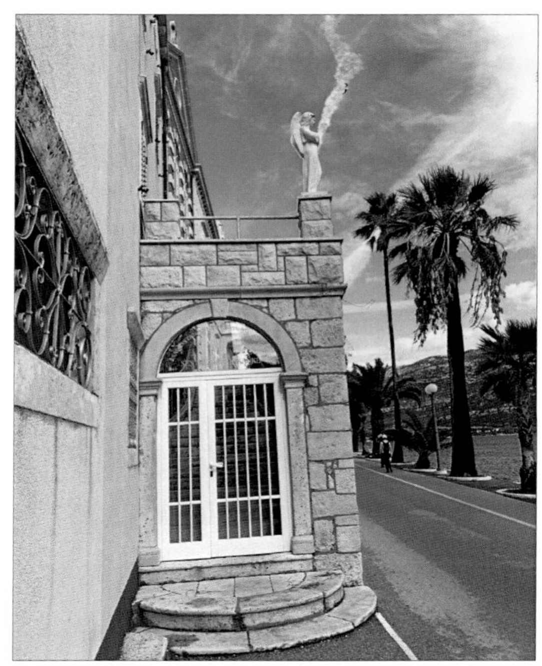

The door to the monastery

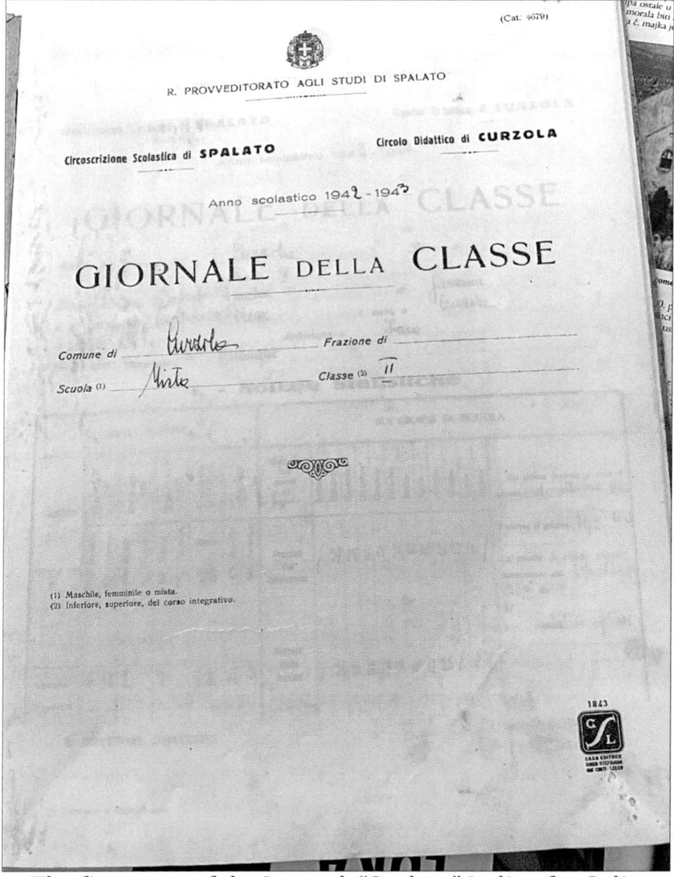

(Cat. 4079)

R. PROVVEDITORATO AGLI STUDI DI SPALATO

Circoscrizione Scolastica di SPALATO

Circolo Didattico di CURZOLA

Anno scolastico 1942 - 1943

GIORNALE DELLA CLASSE

Comune di Curzola	Frazione di
Scuola (1) Mista	Classe (2) II

(1) Maschile, femminile o mista.
(2) Inferiore, superiore, del corso integrativo.

The first page of the Journal. “Spalato” Italian for Split.
“Curzola” Italian for Korčula.
School year written in as 1942-1943

At the state archive office on Korčula, Paul, myself and the archivist were very excited to investigate this oversized Journal to see if it documented my mother’s attendance at school.

The archivest explained that when the Italians occupied the area, they changed the language of the school system to Italian. The nuns had to stop teaching the local students and the Italians opened a school with their own teachers. We were all surprised and delighted to find my mother’s name listed as a student.

II. - Elenco degli alunni della Classe II Privatisti.

N. d'ordine	COGNOME e NOME degli alunni (in ordine alfabetico)	Paternità	Maternità	Comune di nascita	Data di nascita
1	Alkalaj Giorgina	f. Moze	Pressburger Greta	Zagabria (Croazia)	10 Giugno 1935
2	Arnstein Eva	f. Lavoslav	f. Elena Ackermann	Zagabria Croazia	14 luglio 1935
3	Bokros Maira	f. Filippo	f. Alice Reich	Belgrado (Croazia)	13 dicembre 1935
4	Brandu Anna	f. Isidoro	f. Fanny Elle	Sarajevo (Croazia)	28 luglio 1934
5	Gaon Bianca	f. Alberto	f. Grazia Levi	Zagabria (Croazia)	23 ottobre 1935
6	Vesel Anna	f. Giuseppe	f. Hofbauer Mela	Sarajevo (Croazia)	21 ottobre 1934

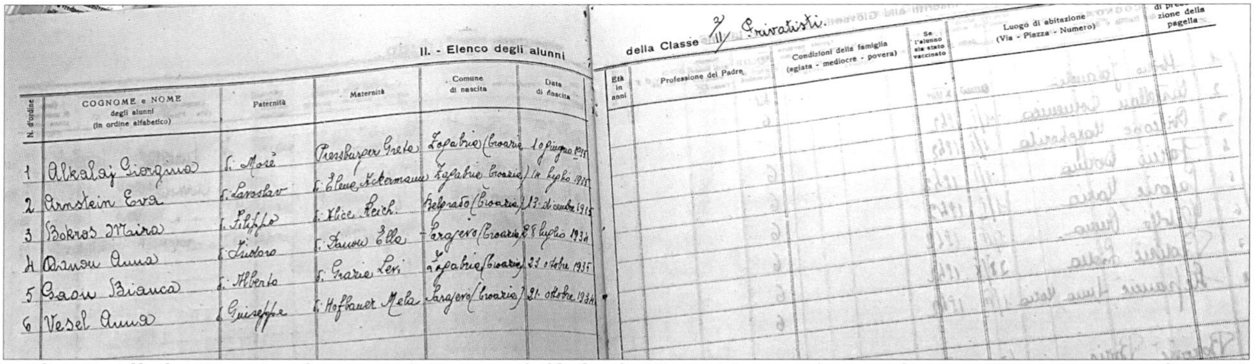

Number 1: Alkalaj Giorgina (my mom). Paternità (father): Moze, Maternità: Pressburger Greta, Comune di nascita (birthplace): Zagabria, Croazia (Zagreb, Croatia), Data di nascita (Date of birth): 10 Giugno (June) 1935.

Esami degli alunni privatisti

Numero progressivo	COGNOME e NOME dell' alunno	Scuola da cui proviene	Paternità	Cognome e Nome della madre	Comune e data di nascita	Assenze: Giustificate	Non giustificate	Totale
1	Alkalaj Giorgina	Privata	f. Mosè	f. Pressburger Greta	Zagabria 10-6-1935			
2	Arnstein Eva	"	f. Ladislav	f. Ackermann Elena	Zagabria 14-7-1935			
3	Boros Mira	"	f. Filippo	f. Reich Alice	Belgrado 13-12-1935			
4	Danon Anna	"	f. Isidoro	f. Danon Elle	Serajevo 28-7-1934			
5	Gaon Bianca	"	f. Alberto	f. Levi Grazia	Zagabria 23-10-1935			
6	Vesel Anna	"	f. Giuseppe	f. Hofbauer Mela	Serajevo 21-10-1934			

MATERIE D'ESAME — Voto annuo di profitto assegnato all' alunno dalla Commissione esaminatrice

No.	Voti (Materie d'esame)	RISULTATO FINALE degli scrutini e degli esami	Osservazioni
1	buono, suff, buono, buono, buono, buono, buono, buono	Approvate	
2	buono, buono, buono, buono, buono, buono, buono, buono	"	
3	buono, buono, buono, buono, buono, buono, buono, buono	"	
4	suff., buono, buono, buono, buono, buono, buono, buono	"	
5	lod., buono, buono, buono, buono, buono, buono, buono	"	
6	lod., lod., lod., lod., lod., lod., buono, buono	"	

Grades posted on the right, mostly "bueno"

The archivist noted that the Jews are listed as private students. He believed these students were taught by the nuns and came to the school only to take exams.

My mother enjoyed attending this school, though she recalls one particularly awkward communion procession:

> *I was wearing a white dress. We were lined up behind the nuns. I was directly behind a nun who, as nuns do, was wearing a long flowing black habit. The children were each holding a candle. The flame on my candle suddenly lit the habit of the nun I was following and set the cloth on fire. The nuns thought I did this on purpose. My punishment was to kneel on dried corn kernels scattered on the floor.*

Childhood memories of foods might include your mom's classic Hungarian Paprikash, or for us growing up it was peanut butter and Fluffernutter sandwiches. For my mother, talk about wartime shortages of available foods brought up disgusting food memories and avoidance methods. In Korčula, for example:

> *I hid pieces of bread, smothered with thick lard, inside a trunk. Blood sausage, bought from Mr. Laterer, that especially went into the trunk. One day, my mother needed to get into this trunk where I had hidden the sandwiches. I sat on top of the trunk and wouldn't let her open it. She wasn't very happy with me. You see, Blood sausage made of blood and sawdust was very expensive and hard to get. My mom figured it was a healthy meal for me.*

Mr. Laterer, the butcher, also sold Greta a collection of stamps which he claimed would some day be worth a fortune. My mother still has this collection, its value is undetermined.

On Korčula, Greta and my mom were eventually joined by her sister, Zelma and her two children

Ellie and Nandi. Ellie was 18. She was interested in dance and acting and was able to bring some of her ballet clothes with her. My mom remembers a day when she tried on her cousin's ballet clothes and danced around an amphitheater. Memorable perhaps, because this little girl of seven, had a moment to escape the uncertainties of life, the fears, and the disruption of her childhood to plié and dance to an imaginary crowd and hear their grand applause.

Ellie's boyfriend, who wasn't Jewish, participated in the Partisans' actions. Ellie may also have participated. They saw each other in between Partisan activities. Mom remembers Ellie's boyfriend taking good care of her when he visited. Unfortunately, he was caught by the Italian army. Ellie and Greta tried to get him released but were unsuccessful. He was taken to a graveyard and killed. Ellie and Greta stood outside the gate and watched. For the rest of her life, my mother would reflect on this sad event, imagining what it must have been like for these two women to witness the murder of their beloved young man.

Ellie's brother, Nandi, also joined the Partisans. One mystery for my mother is how Ellie and Nandi seemed to disappear from the internment camp and avoid check-ins on Fridays. Every Friday, the Italians provided a fish dinner, as part of the check-in. She remembers entering through a nice gate and you checked in with your booklet confirming your whereabouts.

Unfortunately, while fighting with the Partisans Nandi was shot in the leg near the thigh. The wound became infected and he lost his leg above the knee. Without proper medical supplies, he was knocked out with alcohol and the leg sawed off. It festered with sores for years and eventually would need to be reduced higher, leaving a stump.

Greta was able to visit Nandi at the hospital, in an Italian occupied section of Yugoslavia. She brought him a leather writing folder with paper and pens. It turns out, this leather folder belonged to my mother. Apparently, Greta never explained what she did, and my mother never figured out how her leather folder disappeared. Years later, after emigrating to Israel, my mother had the opportunity to visit Nandi in Nahariya, where he had emigrated. There, in Nandi's home, she spotted the leather folder. Greta's secretiveness sometimes left my mother scared, mad, or just confused — she wished her mother had just told her that she had given the folder to Nandi.

Another secret involved Greta trying to save a person suspected of being in the Partisans. Somehow Greta knew he was not involved, and she needed to get to the authorities on another of the coastal islands. Since Aunt Zelma had not yet arrived, Greta needed a safe place to leave my mother while she was away helping this person. Greta brought little Djurdjica (my mom) to a vineyard where she was left with the farmers. Here again, my mother has a vivid memory because she was scared:

> *We walked up a big hill. I remember holding my mother's hand and when I got too tired she carried me on her back. My mother thought I would be safe, but some bombs fell so near, they scared the living daylights out of me. I don't know why she left me with the farmers.*

Even though she eventually learned that her mother had to help someone, my mother never heard more of who or what this was all about, which leaves her still confused and unsettled in her voice as she reflects:

There were other times when my mother left me alone on the island, but by then Zelma had arrived. I missed my mother and was lonely when she was gone, but I wasn't as scared as that time on the mountain!

There is a page in my mother's passport from the Kingdom of Yugoslavia which is interesting.

In bold capital letters, at the top it says: POSLANSTVO KRALJEVINE JUGOSLAVIJE (Croatian) and LEGATION ROYALE DE YOUGOSLAVIE (French)

Which translates to: Mission (Consulate) of the Kingdom of Yugoslavia

Then in French: La validité du present passeport est prolongée jusqu'au: 31 Dec. 1943

Which translates to: The valididty of this passport is extended until 31 Dec. 1943

The next French lines translate to: Valid to travel to France, Spain, Portugal, Great Britain and to overseas countries, meaning territories belonging to the countries listed.

Berne, 9 Feb. 1943 (Berne, Switzerland)

With a stamp of Légation Royale de Yougoslavie en Suisse

Feb. 1943, my mom was on the Island of Korčula. So, what is this entry all about?

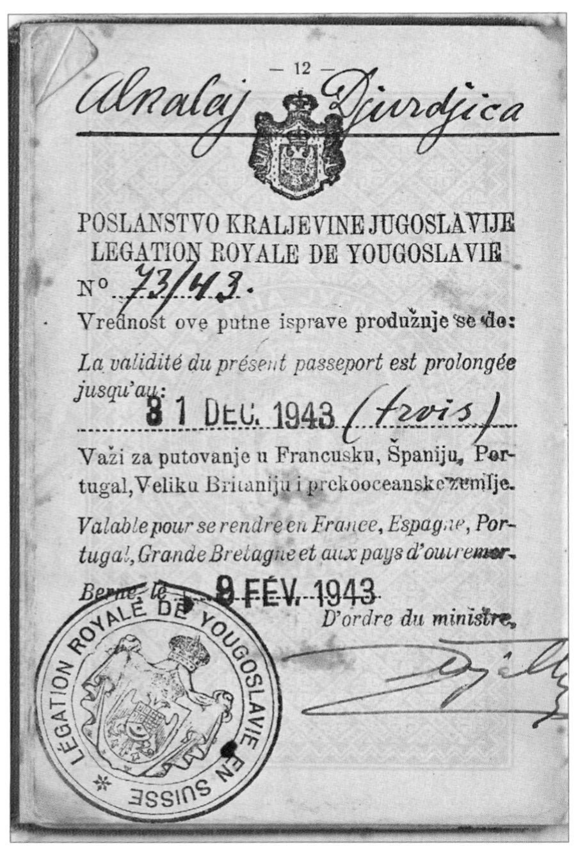

— 12 —

Alkalaj Djurdjica

POSLANSTVO KRALJEVINE JUGOSLAVIJE
LEGATION ROYALE DE YOUGOSLAVIE
N° 73/43.

Vrednost ove putne isprave produžuje se do:

La validité du présent passeport est prolongée jusqu'au:

31 DEC. 1943 (trois)

Važi za putovanje u Francusku, Španiju, Portugal, Veliku Britaniju i prekooceanske zemlje.

Valable pour se rendre en France, Espagne, Portugal, Grande Bretagne et aux pays d'outremer.

Berne, le 9 FÉV. 1943

D'ordre du ministre,

LÉGATION ROYALE DE YOUGOSLAVIE EN SUISSE

Passport page 12 of Alkalaj Djurdjica

A possible explanation comes from Milan Koljanin, in his research, *Escape From the Holocaust. Yugoslav Jews in Switzerland (1941-1945).* Koljanin writes that Jews fleeing from Croatia to the Italian controlled territory lacked proper travel documents. The Italian authorities resolved this by working with the Yugoslav government-in-exile, the former Yugoslav government leaders who had fled to Switzerland, when the Germans invaded. This organization certified travel documents and extended passports for the Yugoslav Jews. This raises the question of why the Italians bothered with this. According to Koljianin, the Italian authorities, with influence from the Vatican, may have intended to move the Jews to other countries, beyond the reach of the Croatian Ustasha and the Germans.[5]

Perhaps, Greta and my mother may have eventually left for one of the countries mentioned in her Passport on page 12, however on September 8th, 1943 the Italians surrendered (capitulated) to the Allies and their lives once again suddenly changed.

5 MILAN KOLJANIN Institute for Contemporary History Belgrade mbkoljanin@gmail.com
ESCAPE FROM THE HOLOCAUST. YUGOSLAV JEWS IN SWITZERLAND (1941-1945)

Korčula to Bari – Another Escape

Why did the Italians capitulate? The war had been going on for four years. The tide had turned against Germany and their Axis allies. In the east, the Soviet Union was pushing back the German forces. The Italians, under Mussolini, who had built an army with over a million men, started to see defeats in Greece, Egypt, and North Africa. By 1942, Italy was dependent on Nazi Germany. Finally, in July 1943, the Allies took control of Sicily which gave them easy access to Italy. On September 3, 1943 the Allies begin their attacks and movement into Italy. The United States and Britain battled the Germans, who retreated to the Northern areas of Italy which they controlled. The southern part of Italy was now controlled by Britain and the United States. Bari is located on the south east coast of Italy.

With the capitulation of the Italians, the Jewish refugees and the Italian soldiers on Korčula, were no longer in safe territory. The Germans were ready to take over the Dalmatian Coast and Korćula. The Germans were also fighting the Partisans. The Partisans tried to negotiate with the Italians. If the Italians agreed to give them weapons and ammunition, they would give them safe passage to Italy. However, the Italians declined.

Instead, the Italian soldiers decided to escape from Korčula using women and children as cover, hoping to prevent an attack. And so, my mother and Greta left Korčula on a fishing boat with the Italian soldiers. This excerpt comes from my mother's vignettes written in her young voice as Giorgina, about her experience escaping Korčula:

> *We are in Korčula, I am already seven years old. We are preparing to leave with the Italian soldiers to go to Italy on fishing boats. My mom is packing our clothing and other things, but only some of them, because we cannot take any more than one suitcase each. Mine is small and mom's is larger but not very large because we have to be able to carry them ourselves. She tells me to choose two things that I want to take so I look for my red leather-writing notebook – I cannot write yet but I love it. I cannot find it. My aunt is trying to help but she is very upset that we are leaving and she is not. Mom and aunt Zelma are arguing. I am fussing and complaining so mom says she will help look for the notebook when she starts cleaning up the apartment. She will find it for me and I should look for the second thing I can take – and that is a broken watch.*
>
> *We eat fish once a week but most of the time we eat Sholet, which is beans and rice and hambones and also watermelons. My mother thinks I need different, healthy food but she can only get it from some people in their house, like the Blood sausage she buys from Mr. Lederer, and the butter she buys from a woman who has goats. She also buys cod liver oil and Liver Wurst. I hate them all. My mother talks about food a lot and she tries to make me eat, especially the stuff I put in the left side of my mouth and keep it there until I can spit it out. I like the Sholet, watermelons and fish, which we eat once a week in a beach restaurant with the other people who are interned on Korčula. People are friendly and there is music.*

I finally find the broken watch and my mother starts cleaning up. She looks at the large, dark, old trunk in the hall. It has a top and a cushion on it and it is the place where I like to play with my things and talk to my friend who is not there. My mother says I make this up and that it is not honest, but I see my friend and we talk. I sit down on the trunk but my mom says I should get up because she will look in it. I do not want to get up and I tell her the door is very heavy. But she says she wants some of the things in it and I must get up. I feel terrible. I know I have been bad – I have thrown the breads with the thick butter and the blood sausage in the trunk.

I get up and mom opens the top. My aunt Zelma is standing there also which makes me more afraid. When mother opens the trunk, there is a bad smell and she sees the breads and blood sausage. They smell and they are green. My mother and aunt speak in Hungarian, which I do not understand, because I speak German and Yugoslav, and then they are yelling. My mom tells me that she spent our money so that I would have healthy food, so she and my aunt never ate this special food, and I was not telling her the truth, and hiding things from her. I don't know what to say except that I have to throw up when I eat this food. I do not tell her that I throw the slimy breakfast oatmeal into the toilet when she is not looking. I do not remember what happens then except that I see the smelly food is thrown out and I feel bad about it then. So I hug my mother and I think she forgives me. We do not find the little red leather notebook.

"We leave Korčula at night– it is dark, wet, cold and scary. First, we are in the belly of the boats, but later the soldiers put us on deck so we can be seen. Airplanes close over us and shoot at us and I hide behind my mother and wrap my arms around her legs. There is a coffin on the boat and I am afraid it will get shot open. I have never seen a dead person, so I am also very frightened of this. Now we have to get off the boats and walk in the water to another island and hide from the planes under the trees in a field. The island is called Lastavo. I am separated from my mother. I am under a tree with the coffin, and some other people and told not to move. Eventually, we go back on the fishing boat and back to Korčula. At night we leave again. It was very scary.

In telling me about this memory, my mother adds, "I didn't like the casket and that fear and memory lingers today. It's why I do not like to attend funerals." The memory of this scary boat ride was also mentioned in the oral history of Flory Jagoda in the collections at the United States Holocaust Museum. [6]Additionally, in the interview with Bimba Beck, she describes the escapes from Kortúla thus: "It was four months of horrifying escaping from Korčula to Bari on fishing boats. We didn't know where we were going." Eventually, all three women, Zelma, Bimba, and Greta reunite in Bari having arrived on separate fishing boats.

6 Interview with Flory Jagoda: https://collections.ushmm.org/search/catalog/irn504836

BARI, ITALY

DURING THE WAR, Italy established displaced persons and refugee camps. One such camp was at Bari, where Greta and my mother arrived from Korčula. In Bari, mom's name changes to Giulia Alkalaj.

Surname	Alkalaj
First name	Giulia
M / F	F
Paternity	
Birth place	
Nation or Nationality	yugoslav
Date of birth	
relatives	Mother Pressburger Greta
In Italy a	
In Italy from	
Last locality or internment camp found	
province	
Internment course	
Deported / a	No
After the escape and / or release a	Bari 16.08.1944
Sources	**H6** - Lists of former internees present in Bari in AS-BA, ECA fund, b. 259, fasc. 44: "Statement of sums paid for subsidies to former inmates", a.1944
Family identified	Pressburger Filippo (grandfather) - Pressburger Greta (mother) -
Possible related names	

Image from data base of foreign Jews interned in Bari, Italy during the war period. Lists mom as Giulia Alkalaj, her Italian name on entering Bari. Escape and/or Release date of August 16, 1944.

At the refugee camp, immigrants were sprayed with a disinfectant called FLIT. In this excerpt from my mother's vignette about Bari, Giulia describes the camp and the moment she is lined up to be sprayed:

Mom and I are now in a large camp for displaced people, in tents and barracks; A muddy, confusing place with people walking in every direction all the time, with lots of rules and regulations, and lots of children. We play hopscotch, jump rope, marbles, jacks, and hide and seek.

One afternoon children are collected into a barrack and I stand in line. I smell something bad and I hear someone crying. Then it is almost my turn and I see a flit gun, which a woman is pumping, and smelly spray goes on the girl in front of me. I feel sick from the spray, I am frightened and suddenly I run away through the door in the back. I find a tree behind a barrack and hide there. I am scared that they will find me and I feel offended that we are sprayed like animals. I stay where I am until my Mother finds me late in the afternoon. I run into her arms and tell her tearfully that some people tried to spray me with a Flit gun. My Mother says that it was to take lice off our bodies, and especially our heads. She tells me not to worry; she knows I do not have lice.

Interestingly, my father points out, "While mom was getting sprayed with FLIT, I was spraying cows with FLIT on the Rewald farm, in Venice Center, New York. The spraying devices were identical and also the chemical agent being sprayed. The only difference was that the cows did not seem to be bothered by the spraying."

FLIT-Insecticide

FLIT is an insecticide used to kill flies and mosquitoes. It contained DDT, which was widely used during WWII to prevent the spread of diseases such as malaria (mosquitoes) and typhoid (fleas). In Italy, towns were dusted from the air with DDT to control lice. In October 1943, when my mother was arriving in Bari, the Allies liberated Naples, where a lice borne typhoid epidemic was occurring. The Americans sprayed soldiers, civilians, and refugees with a powder mixed with 10% DDT, which most likely is what was used on the refugees over in Bari. The spread of typhus was greatly reduced, but thousands of people were exposed to a harmful chemical — just how harmful is still being debated. This cancer-causing pesticide would be banned for agricultural use in the U.S. in 1979 and worldwide in 2004, except in areas where malaria exists.

Over in the United States, as my dad mentions, FLIT became widely used by farmers trying to protect their crops and animals from disease. The famous children's book author Theodor Geisel, better known as Dr. Seuss, worked for FLIT for seventeen years making advertisements with the popular Slogan, "Quick Henry, the FLIT" using his now, well known, drawing style. He also was creating political cartoons such as this one from December 1941, printed in the New York City newspaper, PM, which includes the image of a FLIT spray pump disinfecting Nazi (Hitler) and Japanese (Hirohito) mosquitoes, and an Italian (Mussolini) flea.

The American Pilots

The Americans in Bari needed help recognizing if staff members of the military were actually spies. Therefore, they hired people who spoke many languages. Greta spoke or understood Hungarian, Serbo-Croation, Czech, German, Italian, and English. From my mother's Bari vignette, Giulia describes her mom's interview day:

> *A scary thing happens one day. My mother leaves me to go to town. She does not tell me why, but I see her in an open back truck with other women. She tells me not to worry, that she will be back soon. She is dressed nicely and looks beautiful. Slim. With long dark hair and blue gray eyes and a nice smile.*

My mother, just 8 years old, watched as her mother joined the other women. Greta didn't tell her daughter why she was leaving. "She was secretive in order to protect me which made me scared instead. My mother was a very brave person." This young child, already experienced at how war separates families, felt scared as she watched the truck leave with her mother. There were many scary times for my mother, but here I can picture her standing and watching her mom and the overwhelming sense of loneliness, "Will I see my mother again?" I just want to put my arm around that little girl and reassure her, everything will be OK.

Mom wearing school outfit, holding the doll American pilots gave to her.

The women on the truck were selected to be interviewed at the American headquarters in Bari for a job with General Twining, later to become Chairman of the Joint Chiefs of Staff, of the U.S. Department of Defense. My grandmother Greta was selected to cook breakfast and dinner for five American pilots. These were officers living in the home of an Italian doctor, who, was interned, perhaps at one of the Italian camps. Greta didn't tell her interviewer she had a child, but she arrived at the house with my mother, and the officers agreed to let them both stay. In fact, some of the pilots had children, so my mother was a reminder of their families back home. The pilots gave my mother a doll. Of this memory my mom states:

I was so excited to get this doll. I ran around the house yelling, "Bambola! Bambola!" That is Italian for doll. I had never seen a doll before. I remember a stranger saying, 'only Americans would give you a doll that size!'

Don Middelton was a Pilot in the Canadian air force. My mother fondly remembers him stopping by to take my mom for walks. Don gave my mom a photo of him with a personal message written on the back. She still owns the photo. The back of the photograph says, "To Georgia, with thanks for a very happy time in Bari, 3 April 44, Don" and his signature (see photo).

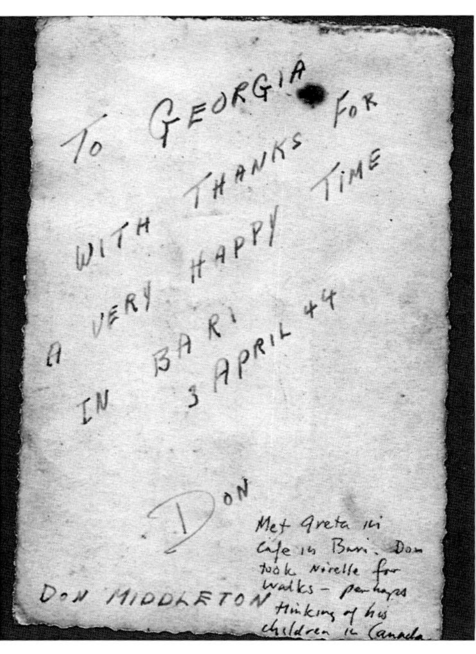

Left: Photograph of Don Middleton, Canadian Airforce. Right: Back of Photo reads: To Georgia, with thanks for a very happy time in Bari. 3 April 44. Don, Don Middleton. (In the corner my father has written a note, "Met Greta in a Café, Pilot from Canada-mom remembers him taking her for walks."

Living with the pilots was better than life in the refugee camp, however it was also lonely as my mom explains through the voice of Giulia in this excerpt from her Vignette about Bari:

I am happy in the apartment – the flyers spoil me with candy and chocolates from the American air base. I am also very lonely, I do not speak almost any Italian, no English, and the Italian children in the neighborhood do not like the Americans. I now know we are in the apartment of an important Italian doctor who has been taken to a camp for Italian prisoners of war.

I like to sit on the balcony and watch the children play soccer in the street. They also jump rope and play tag. One day I am eating candy and I throw some down from the balcony. The children in the street push each other to catch what I am throwing, and I throw some more. They yell at me but I do not understand. I do this for a few more days – my mother sees me and does not like it. She tells me to stop because they will hate me for trying to be more important and better than they are and pretending to be rich when we are really poor. I tell her I am lonely, and I thought the children would play with me. Mother says she will put me in a school – she does – in a convent with huge classes and scary strict nuns who rap me on the knuckles when they think I am not paying attention. They are more scary than the nuns in Korchula.

One of the five American pilots of the 15th Air Force staying at the house was a Major Browning. My mother remembers him fondly and reflecting back believes her mother was in love with him. At some point he was at a hospital. Again, an excerpt in Giulia's voice:

Major Browning tells me to call him Brownie and that he has a daughter in America. Later, Brownie is not around, and I ask my mother where he is. She says she does not know, but one dark afternoon Mother and I hitch hike on army trucks with big headlights, driving in the mud, and arrive at a hospital where we visit Brownie. He looks different – not his body, but he is not looking much at us and he does not talk. I do not understand, and my mother does not explain. We return by hitch hiking on three trucks to get back to our apartment. After that we do not see Brownie anymore, and my mother often cries and tells me she misses him. I think she loves him – I do. She says that he went back to America, and I hope he will invite us there.

The Jewish Brigade

Greta was working and Guilia (mom's Italian name) needed to attend school. Again, Greta felt it was safer for my mother to be at a school with nuns. This was a large school, and unfortunately for my mother, these nuns were not as nice as the ones on Korćula:

The pupils sat lined up in rows, like pews, of twenty kids. The nuns walked around with rulers. Any time you did something wrong you were made to kneel on rice in the corner.

My independent mother, now eight years old, would have none of it and so she rebelled. Excerpt from "Bari" in Giulia's voice:

Soon I pretend to go to school, my mother goes to work, and I go to the harbor. I love the sea, I watch fishermen on the shore dangling their lines, carts full of things, which are lifted onto large ships. There are many very large ships in the harbor. Because I hear English words, I think they are American ships. I like the cobblestones – they are good for hopscotch and I like looking at the soldiers. I have no father at home, and sometimes I think someone looks like him. One day a soldier found me. He gave me a chocolate and asked why I wasn't in school. Then he brought me to my mother. He told her she needs to keep a better eye on her daughter. He told her about a different school in town. Now, I am going to the new school, which is in a home with a garden and with only a few children, boys and girls, of different ages. Soon more children come, one at a time, until there are about 30. We are happy there, and it feels like a family.

The school recommended by the soldier was started by the Jewish Brigade for displaced children. My mom liked this school much better.

School children with the Jewish Brigade, Bari, Italy. Mom in center, with necklace

In this photo of school children with the Jewish Brigade, my mother is standing in the middle of the second row, wearing a necklace, with her friend Ella's arm around her neck. Ella eventually married a friend they both came to know in Israel, Michael Strauss. My mother met and dated Michael at the first school she attended in Nahariya, Israel.

The soldier in the photo is from the Jewish Brigade. He encouraged Greta to go to Israel, even though she already had papers for the United States. He returned to Israel after the war and was killed in an attack on the Tel Aviv airport.

Even though my mother wasn't happy with the nuns, she did like the church and kept visiting it just to, "*sit and enjoy the quiet. It felt safe, smelled nice and wasn't cold.*"

Who was the Jewish Brigade? After WWI Great Britain controlled Palestine and was issued the British Mandate to work with the Arabs and Jewish population with the intention of facilitating a Jewish homeland. At the beginning of WWII, Britain needed men to help defend the Middle East. Twelve thousand Palestinians volunteered. Britain also established 25 Jewish Brigades. Both the Palestinians and the Jewish Brigades helped fight in Greece, Egypt, and Northern Africa. When Italy capitulated, there were 5,000 men in the Jewish Brigade stationed along the border with Austria and Yugoslavia. They helped the Allies fight the Germans until the end of the war and were eventually disbanded in 1946. Some of these soldiers helped create camps for Jewish displaced persons and also encouraged their resettlement to Palestine.

The "Pearl Harbor of Italy" and Chemotherapy

At one of our family gatherings my mother told us this war story:

> *We stayed in the home once belonging to a Doctor. There was a full human skeleton in a small room, which once served as a doctor's office, which scared me. And, in the kitchen, my mother would line up eggs on a window sill. Well one day, there was a terrible bombing in the port at Bari and all those eggs went flying and made a terrible mess and that scary skeleton shattered!*

There was relief in her voice, that this scary skeleton was broken apart - and we family members laughed. My mother was suddenly taken aback by our laughter and said:

> *It wasn't funny at all, it was a very bad day. The blast was so large the men on the roof were blown back and many people died.*

My mother was referring to the "Pearl Harbor of Italy." The British in control of the harbor were convinced the Germans did not have the fire power to attack the port. Yet, on December 2, 1943 the port at Bari was unexpectedly bombed by the Germans. Twenty-nine military ships were docked there loaded or preparing to load up with bombs, ammunition, aviation fuel, hospital equipment and military supplies. As a result, the explosions were massive. In particular, one ship, the John Harvey, had an explosion which rattled the entire harbor, set other boats in flames, and tossed people and shards of metal 30 feet into the air. The John Harvey was carrying a secret cargo - 100 tons of mustard gas. Even though the United States would not use poisonous gas, they were prepared to retaliate if the enemy used chemical warfare on the Allies. This ship and sixteen other ships were destroyed, and 8 ships were damaged. One thousand people died and 617, probably more, were exposed to mustard gas.

Lieutenant Colonel Stewart Francis Alexander was assigned to investigate the strange illness that soldiers and people living in the city were sickened and dying from. As a chemist, he was able to identify the cause as mustard gas. However, the Prime Minister of Britain, Winston Churchill and the U.S. General Dwight Eisenhower, kept the mustard gas censored.

Out of horror came a valuable chemotherapy treatment. Alexander's boss, Colonel Cornelius P. Rhoads, recognized the effects of mustard gas on cell division. He then worked with General Motors' Alfred P. Sloane and Charles F. Kettering to finance cancer research, establishing the renowned Sloan Kettering Institute. The research on nitrogen mustard led to the first FDA approved chemotherapy. This first treatment was used on patients with non-Hodgkin's lymphoma.

Marlene Dietrich

Imagine you are a beautiful woman with an interest in fashion and theater, but you are currently a refugee in a foreign country, working as a cook when a famous actress comes to visit the officers for whom you work. Greta must have been over the moon with excitement when General Twining asked her to help care for Marlene Dietrich while she stayed in town.

Marlene Dietrich

Mary Magdelene "Marlene" Dietrich (1901-1992) was an actress from Germany who became a famous American movie actress. She became a U.S. citizen in 1939. After the Japanese attack on Pearl Harbor she sold U.S. war bonds raising nearly one million dollars. The Nazi government tried to persuade her to return to Germany to help the war effort there, but she refused which put her on Hitler's list of traitors. She is also well known for her participation in the United Service Organization (USO) tours of entertainers visiting the troops. Dietrich performed for the Allied troops in Italy, Britian, France, Belgium and Algeria. She made over 500 USO appearances singing, dancing, entertaining the troops as well as visiting the sick. She was a whirlwind of energy and strength under extreme circumstances and the soldiers were grateful. Dietrich was given the U.S. Medal of Freedom in 1945 for her war efforts.

Her talent was also used by the U.S. Office of Strategic Services (which became the CIA) as part of their Morale Operations Branch. Their mission was to create propaganda to lower the morale of German troops and to create discord with the Italians and Fascists. The OSS MUZAK project broadcasted "black" radio programs. "Black propaganda" is meant to influence the listeners without them realizing who actually is behind the program. Soldatensender (soldiers' Radio) was the most popular radio program in Germany. Marlene Dietrich, Bing Crosby and Dina Shore recorded songs for Soldatensender in German and English. The song "Lili Marlene" sung by Dietrich became so popular, the Nazi government banned it temporarily. The U.S. military found these musical broadcasts effective at changing attitudes amongst civilian and German military personnel towards the Nazi regime.

In order to attend to Marlene's personal needs, Greta moved in with her at a beautiful high-rise apartment. By then cousin Ellie had arrived in Bari also. Assisting with Marlene meant Greta had access to her bedroom. I can imagine myself peeking in Marlene's room and desiring to try on her fancy jewelry and clothing in front of a mirror. Well, that is exactly what Greta and Ellie managed to do. My mother was told to keep watch outside the room, while Greta and her niece tried on Marlene's clothes and used her makeup. Mom did get a chance too, trying on Marlene's fake eyelashes. I wish there was a photo of that!

Apparently, Marlene would wear certain head bands or scarves depending on which foreign officers she might greet. She would choose scarves in the appropriate colors of their countries to send a secret message. One time she asked Greta to help write in Russian (which is similar to Serbian) the words, "I love you" or "Ja the ljublju," before meeting a Russian general. Of Marlene, my mother recalls:

> *One time, a stranger asked me about Marlene. He was an elevator operator who asked 'How are her legs?' I was 8 years old and had no idea what he was talking about. Then one day, when I was taking a bath, in walks Marlene Dietrich and asks if she can join me.*

My mother adds, with a giggle:

> *Once she was settled into the tub, I got scared and got out right away because actually, I was afraid of her legs!*

However, my mother noted that, "Marlene was extremely nice to me because she missed her daughter back home."

While in Bari in 1943, Marlene became sick with pneumonia. She had worn herself out and was ordered to the hospital by army doctors. She received the newly invented penicillin which probably saved her life. At the time, penicillin was still in the experimental stage and not yet available to the general public. Only the wealthy had access to this new trial drug. The British scientists, Fleming, Florey and Chain, were struggling to grow enough penicillin. A lab in Illinois run by Andrew Moyer developed a technique to mass produce penicillin. Beer enthusiasts might be interested to learn that he used beer vats to grow larger quantities of penicillin. In 1943, penicillin powder was being experimented with on soldiers' wounds fighting in North Africa. Luckily, the military in Bari also had some penicillin on hand. By the end of the war, penicillin would be accepted as a miracle cure and widely available in the U.S. Fleming, Florey, and Chain were awarded a Medicine Nobel Prize in 1945.

In 1962 Marlene toured Israel and took time to visit Greta. During this tour Israel gave her the Israeli Medallion of Valor honoring her "friendship for the Jewish people." Marlene renounced her German citizenship. Furthermore, she had a difficult reception when she eventually toured Germany and distanced herself from her sister who ran a cinema visited by Nazi officials overseeing the Bergen-Belsen concentration camp. Nevertheless, Dietrich asked to be buried near the family plot in Berlin.

Marlene was lucky to receive penicillin at a time when disease was as much a threat to humans as wars. For instance, my mother's aunt Sabine (1901-1925) suffered from rheumatic fever at the age of twelve and died from its lingering effects when she was twenty-four years old. In the United

States during the 1920's, rheumatic fever was the leading cause of death for people ages 5 to 20 years old. It affects the heart, joints, and nervous symptoms. Sabine probably was sick for weeks or months and may have had rheumatic heart disease and failure, leading to her death. Seventeen years later, in March 1942, a young woman at New Haven Hospital, Connecticut with rheumatic fever was treated successfully with penicillin. Her hospital chart can be seen at the Smithsonian Institution. Unfortunately, rheumatic fever still exists in places with poverty and lack of access to antibiotics.

Rheumatic fever was described by Hippocrates in the 5th century BCE. Hippocrates was a Greek physician considered the "father of medicine." He also described another disease he called "phthisis," but it was also known as "tabes" to Romans, "schachepheth" in ancient Hebrew, "consumption," "the white plague," "Captain of all these men of death," "graveyard cough," "lung disease," "wasting disease," "the Bugs," and many other nicknames, but today is known as "tuberculosis" or "TB." It's not surprising there are so many nicknames for disease, given that scientists estimate it has been around for three million years.

My mother's grandfather, Fulop Pressburger (1862-1915), died from TB at the age of 53. He probably caught it from someone, just like one might catch the common cold today. The disease was one of the leading causes of death around the world. It could take years to cure, and once identified it took years to come up with an effective treatment. By 1960 doctors finally sorted out the best treatment. Even today there are drug resistant strains of TB, so it remains a serious threat in some parts of the world.

Two of Greta's brothers died very young from the Spanish flu. This disease got its name during WWI when many countries had instituted news censorship, including information about the flu pandemic. However, Spain was neutral during WWI and was free to distribute the information, hence it became known as the Spanish flu. The flu affected an estimated 40% of the global population, killing twice as many as those who died in the war.

And, one more story from mom's time in Bari – *The Fox*. Every so often, as I work on this manuscript, new stories come up. Greta was a single parent, so as mentioned, there are times she leaves my mother with strangers. Each time it is scary for my mom and memorable even after all these years. The fox helped her remember this particular time in Bari:

> *One time my mom left me to live with a fisherman. I was scared to death to go. This fisherman had a daughter much younger than me. The house had little crosses all over the house. I didn't like being there. He also had a "pet" fox which lived in a den behind a fence connected to the house. I had to feed the fox. I like animals, but I did think this was a strange pet!"*

Fisherman's daughter and my mom

Bari to Palestine

Why was it safe to think about leaving Bari? How did Greta decide where to go after Italy? Looking closely at this life changing moment, I can't imagine being in Greta's shoes. All the brave moments that brought her and my mother to the safety of Bari surely gave her strength and resolve for this next change in their lives. It had been just over three years since Buki, Greta, and mom left Zagreb for Sarajevo. Greta didn't know if her husband survived the war, though she told me that while traveling to Split she had a moment when she felt Buki had died.

Two sisters, Greta and Zelma, living in Bari, had to decide where to go next. Two sisters who lost their husbands and with children to care for, must have desired family, friends, and stability. Sisters Ida[7] and Frici were in London. It is unclear where her sister Ilona was at this moment. Her sister Sari has died.

One of the American flyers, with whom Greta and my mother lived, provided a visa for the United States, and encouraged immigration. Perhaps staying in Italy was an option. Zelma with older children, must have pushed for returning to Yugoslavia, as that is where she eventually went. Greta knew that some of Buki's relatives were in Palestine. She was probably aware of friends, such as Karl Moster, who were in Palestine. My mother remembers her mother and Zelma talking in Hungarian, to be private, but she overheard the soldier from the Jewish Brigade, who was teaching at the school, tell Greta that, "a Jewish woman, traveling alone with a child, should go to Palestine." What a huge decision this was for Greta and her nine year old daughter!

Memories and explanations differ between Greta and my mother. Greta told me she decided on Palestine because that is where her daughter wanted to go. My mother remembers it differently. Palestine is where her mother wanted to go. I learned from Olive Silverstein, my mother-in-law, that, "You make the best decision you can with the information you have at that moment." Which means you can't look back and regret because now you have more information that might have influenced the decision. Moving to Palestine brought more difficulties and worries of new wars. For many Jews, Palestine was the only choice, a future homeland. For Greta, Palestine was a destination with family and friends. Recently, my mother reflected that her mom was anxious about going to a place that was unsettled, a newly forming country. Greta never liked the heat and missed her European culture.

Millions of Europeans were displaced during WWII. Most were repatriated. But returning to countries where anti-Semitism thrived was a risky option for Jews. Those that made their way home found little to no community for support. Some were murdered.

So it was, that in March 1945 — one month before Germany surrendered and Hitler committed suicide — Greta and mom made their way to British Palestine.

The boat from Bari carrying Greta and mom might have been a British or American troop boat which also took some Jews whose passage was organized by the Jewish Brigade. The trip to Palestine took about a week. My mom remembered a dining room with columns, which had hammocks hung between them where they slept. When I asked my mother about her memories of this trip, she reflected:

---

7 Ida worked in Vienna. She was the first woman correspondent for Reuters Newspaper. She was told the Gestapo was looking for her in Vienna and not to go home to her apartment. She was advised as well, not to return to Hungary. So, she went to England.

I trusted the Jewish Brigade. I believe I probably thought it was fun and exciting, given my love of boats and my independent nature. I wasn't a scared child. I was scared when my mother left me alone, but otherwise, I was fine. I do remember, on our arrival, my mom found a scorpion in her shoe and I was afraid ever since of scorpions!

PALESTINE

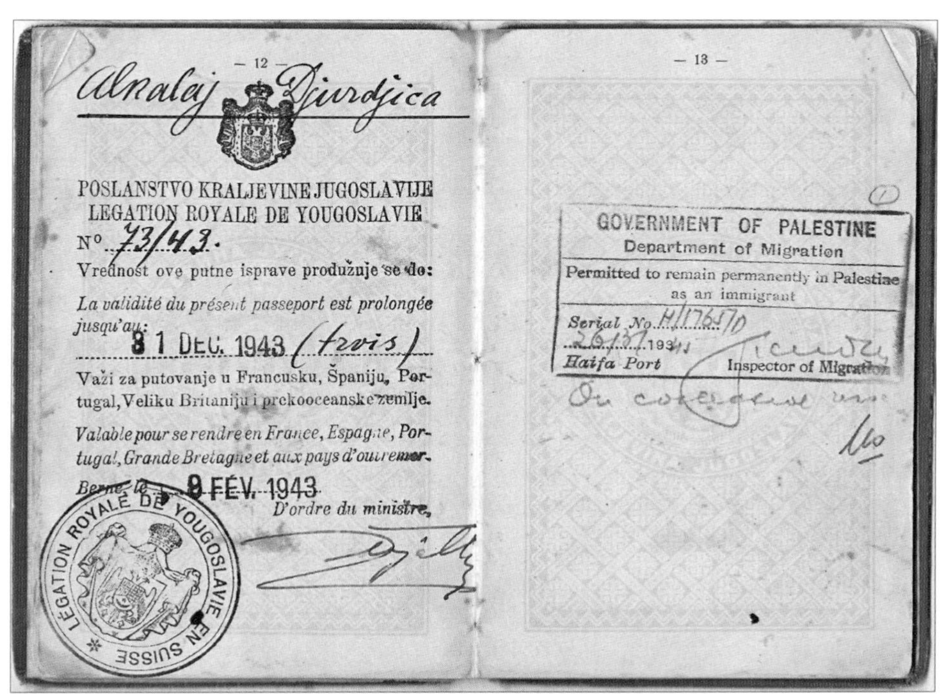

— 12 —

Alkalaj Djurdjica

POSLANSTVO KRALJEVINE JUGOSLAVIJE
LEGATION ROYALE DE YOUGOSLAVIE
No 73/43.

Vrednost ove putne isprave produžuje se do:
La validité du présent passeport est prolongée jusqu'au:
31 DEC. 1943 (trois)

Važi za putovanje u Francusku, Španiju, Portugal, Veliku Britaniju i prekooceanske zemlje.
Valable pour se rendre en France, Espagne, Portugal, Grande Bretagne et aux pays d'outremer.

Berne, le 9 FÉV. 1943
D'ordre du ministre,

LÉGATION ROYALE DE YOUGOSLAVIE EN SUISSE

— 13 —

GOVERNMENT OF PALESTINE
Department of Migration
Permitted to remain permanently in Palestine as an immigrant
Serial No.
Haifa Port — Inspector of Migration

Mom's Passport, page 13: March 26, 1945

Greta and Djurdjica arrived at the Haifa port, in British Palestine, and remained at the Atlit Detainee camp run by the British authorities. Lists of illegal immigrants arriving were published. Greta's sister-in-law, Erna Ascoli (Buki's sister) came looking for relatives. She found Greta and my mom and secured their release.

Once again, my mother and her mom were lucky to get to safety. Lucky to make it safely to Korčula, lucky to make it safely to Bari, lucky to make it safely to Palestine. In 1945, the British allowed only 1,500 immigrants each month, when hundreds of thousands were looking for a safe place to call home. Once the limit was reached, the British were stopping ships and bringing the immigrants to internment camps on Cyprus and to Atlit. Thousands of displaced persons attempted to enter Palestine until 1948, when Palestine became Israel and legal immigration began.

Until then, in the dark of night, illegal immigrants were snuck into Palestine with the help of the Jewish Brigade and the Haganah, a Jewish militia. My mother and Greta could easily have wound up with other illegal immigrants on the island of Cyprus, drowned at sea, or sent back to where they just traveled from. Luckily, in Bari, the Italians and the Americans did not inspect ships leaving. My mom recalls that she was on the last legal ship to arrive in Palestine, perhaps just within the limit allowed for immigrants.

In Palestine, Greta and my mom learn what happened to Buki and to other family members. From a survivor they learned that Buki was killed by the Ustashi at the Jasenovac Concentration Camp. I can only imagine that hearing of these events, the answer to the mystery of what happened to Buki, must have been a moment of closure for Greta, providing both the relief for knowing as well as of grief for her husband.

They also learned that Buki's mother, Hannah died at the Jasenovac concentration camp. And, that Buki's brother Silvio, his wife Ibi and their daughter Leonida also died at concentration camps. Here is what my mother heard about Ibi and Leonida:

> *Ibi and Leonida were entering a concentration camp (possibly Stara Gradiska, a camp for woman with children). Ibi was beautiful and amazingly someone felt sorry for them and let them go. They escaped to a city in Hungary where they were not rounding up Jews. Sadly, close to the end of the war, they were again caught. Ibi did not want to be separated from her child, so they were both sent to the crematorium. The photo of Leonida really upsets me the most. How could they do such a thing to a child. I think about her mom holding her. Can you imagine? That is why I don't like to do those talks at the schools. It's too difficult to think about those things. You want to put it aside and focus on the positives. Now it feels good to talk about it. You need to let it out too."*

Ibi (Silvio's wife/Buki's sister-in-law) and Silvio

Ibi was married to Silvio, Buki's brother. Silvio died at the Jasenovac concentration camp. He is mentioned in the testimony by a witness and survivor of Jasenovac, Slavko Vasic. Vasic provides a detailed description of Jasenovac in the article, "Jasenovac Camp No. IV – Leather Shop." The leather shop was a safer living environment for the Jews at Jasenovac than their desperate life at the other camps. So, the Jews in charge of the factory encouraged the regime to expand the operations. Vasic says that Silvio was allowed to set up a workshop to manufacture fur goods, which became known as the "Alkalaj camps." Other such crafts were established at the factory and in this way, many Jews were rescued from the horrible conditions in the other camps. Near the end of the war, the Ustashi were destroying evidence and killing survivors at the camps. Fearing for their lives, the men at the factory organized an escape. On April 21-22, 1945 six hundred men made an attempt to escape, but only 54 survived. From the tannery, only nine survived. Our family understanding of what happened to Silvio is that:

Silvio had an injury from his days as a footballer and could not run fast enough, so he was shot.

Most were shot as they ran, but in his testimony Vasic states that the detainees also had made some cyanide. He isn't clear if the poison is for the guards or for themselves, however he goes on to state, "...the engineer, Avram Demajo, had made some cyanide and in this way, along with others, the detainee Alkalaj and the engineer Demajo ended." Vasic implies here that Silvio perhaps died from taking cyanide. Whichever way Silvio died it remains evident that he is remembered as a leader who cared for and saved the lives of many Jews during their detention at Jasenovac.

Silvio was an accomplished footballer. He is mentioned in several articles as a coach (the first coach) for the Željezničar, a team formed in 1921with players of the Sarajevo Railway workers. These "Railway Men" became a well-known team that still exists today.

Greta also learns that her sister, Shari/Sari died in Budapest, 1944-45. She gassed herself at home because she was afraid to go to the Gestapo, from where her husband, Eugene Werner, had failed to return.

However, with all this sad news, Greta moves on with her life in Palestine. From the detention center in Haifa they first go to relatives in Ramat Gan.

Sari Pressburger

(L-R) Shari, Ellie, Zelma, Nandi with toy gun, Sabataj, Ida, Greta lying down in front

<u>Djurdjica Turns Ten</u>

Greta and my mom lived with Aunt Erna (Buki's sister) and Uncle Bruno and their four daughters: Hannah, Beba, Rachel, and Leah. Below is a photo of Rachel (who my mom felt was the most friendly of the four children) with Mom who is holding a kitten. Talking about the photo with the kitten, my mom said to me, "Do you see this photo? Look at my face."

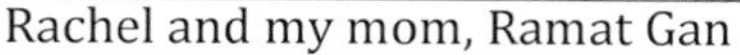
Rachel and my mom, Ramat Gan

Mom and Cousins, Hannah, Beba, and Leah, Ramat Gan

This photo [on the left] really shows how I felt at the time. I was mad. I felt ignored by the family. I didn't like the food, especially the soft- boiled eggs and they would yell at me. On my first day of school, my mother couldn't go with me. I went with Leah. She went into the school and left me outside. I stood outside and never went in. I was terrified. I didn't know the language. I was scared. Back at the house, my mom was mad at me because I wouldn't eat. I sat on the couch and pressed my face between the pillows until I passed out. I was out for five days. When I came to, there was a doctor sitting next to me. Apparently, I had inflammation around the brain. The kitten was a stray cat. I was pretty lonesome, so they let me keep the kitten.

At some point, Greta and my mom moved from Ramat Gan to Tel Aviv. Greta applies for succession of Buki's estate. I found the following notice for Buki's estate in the *Palestine Gazette*, (Published by Authority, No. 1487, Thursday, 11th April 1946, page 362.)

Registrar, District Court, Tel Aviv.

V I I I .

IN THE DISTRICT COURT OF T E L AVIV.

P r o b a t e Case N o . 216/46.
In the matter of the succession to Buki Alkalaj,
late of Zagreb, Yugoslavia, deceased.
P e t i t i o n e r : Greta Alkalaj of Tel Aviv,
through her attorney Dr. Yoel Rosenberger,
advocate of 103, Allenby Street, Tel Aviv.

Let all persons take notice that Greta Alkalaj
of Tel Aviv, Palestine, has applied to the
District Court of Tel Aviv for an order declaring
succession to the estate of Buki Alkalaj,
deceased, and that the said application will
be heard at the District Court of Tel Aviv on
the 21st day of April, 1946, at 9 a.m.
All persons claiming any interest must appear
at the said place and time, otherwise such
order will be made as to the Court seems right.
Dated this 5th day of April. 1946.
E. MANI
(Gaz/18/40) Acting Registrar, District Court, Tel Aviv

Interestingly, in the same Gazette, on page 366, a petition for Greta to have guardianship of Gjurgjica Alkalaj, a minor, was listed. Greta needed a court order to obtain guardianship of her own daughter because the law at the time decreed that the father had guardianship and could appoint in his will a guardian, should he die. In this case, the mother would become a co-guardian who must follow the wishes of the other guardian in terms of decisions about education and religion. It wasn't until the Guardian Act of 1973 (Britian) that women gained full control.

Palestine Gazette, Registrar, District Court, Tel Aviv., page 366.
VI.
IN THE DISTRICT COURT OF TEL AVIV.
P r o b a t e Case N o . 2 1 7 / 4 6 .
In the matter of the appointment of a
guardian over the person and property of
Gjurgjica Alkalaj, a minor.
P e t i t i o n e r : Greta Alkalaj of Tel Aviv,
through her attorney Dr. Yoel Rosenberger,
103, Allenby Street, Tel Aviv.
In virtue of an order of the District Court

of Tel Aviv, bearing date this day, I do hereby cite all and all manner of persons to appear in the said Court in ten days from the date of publication hereof, and show cause, if any they have, why an order appointing the said petitioner guardian over the person and property of Gjurgjica Alkalaj, the minor daughter of Buki Alkalaj, deceased, should not be made, as, in default thereof, such order will be made as to the Court seems right.
Dated this 5th day of A p r i l, 1946.
E. MANI
(Gaz/18/40) Acting Registrar, District Court. Tel Aviv

"I turned ten in Israel," my mother says, as if it is a time stamp in her memory passport:

> *I was in a new country with a new language. Until now, my education in school was taught in Italian. I was speaking Croatian with my mother and had learned quite a bit of English in Italy. Hebrew has a different script and no Indo-European cognates. It was very difficult. However, adapting to new cultures was more difficult than learning languages. There was also some discrimination and a sort of value ranking. Personal traits admired in Korčula were not the same in Palestine. It also felt like I went from one war to another.*

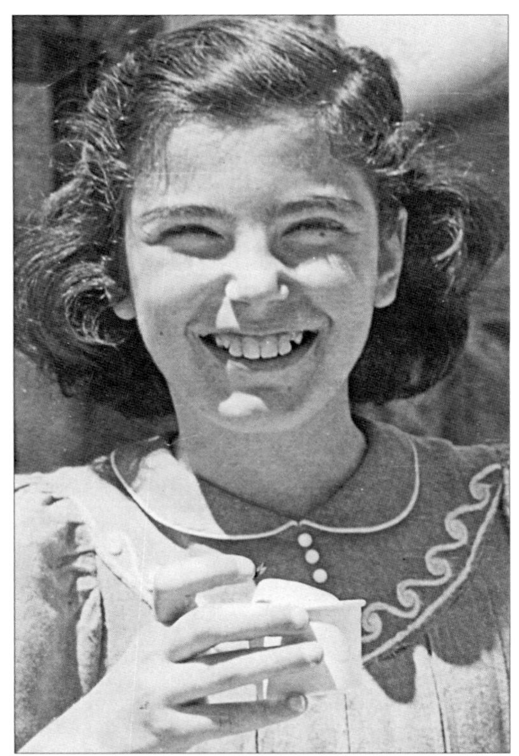
Happy 10th Birthday!

Karl Moster

In addition to a language and culture change, Greta reconnected with a family friend from Yugoslavia, Karl Moster, and they soon married. For my mother, now called Judith, adapting to a new adult authority was probably not easy. And for a while Karl's mother, Hermie, also lived with them. In the end, Karl became a stabilizing figure for the family. He was a loving husband and attentive step-father.

Karl was a bookkeeper and was an active tennis player. He went to Israel as part of the Zionist movement. Karl joined the Haganah to support their effort to create an independent state.

Greta and Mom on the balcony of their apartment on Nordau Street. My mom slept on the balcony and rolled her bed up every day.

Nordau Street, Tel Aviv

Karl and Greta

Karl's father Mavro, and his brother Edmund, had worked with Eduard Penkala to open the "Penkala-Moster" pen and pencil company, well-known for producing the first solid-ink fountain pen. The factory was located in Zagreb and their products sold internationally. Another brother, Bernard, ran a second factory in Berlin. Edmund was killed at Jasenovac, Bernard at Rab concentration camp. The Penkala-Moster factory was taken over by the Yugoslav government and became the "TOZ Company," which still exists. Penkala lived in Croatia and carried on as a well-known inventor.

In an article by the International Leaders Summit in Washington, D.C., *Plight of Croatia's Jews-Restitution of Private Property Blocked by the Balkan Country's Anti-Semitic Laws Mar 16, 2018*, Edmund Moster & Co. in Zagreb is noted as one of the businesses improving economic growth and confiscated by the Ustashi in 1941. The main point of the article is the need for restitution for property owned by the Jewish Community in Croatia.

Karl had a sister, Mary Levine, Aunt Mary. After the war, Mary emigrated to the United States. She worked for the United Nations in New York City as the radio correspondent. She ran the Yugoslav desk where her reporting on world events was broadcast into communist-controlled Yugoslavia.

Penkala logo

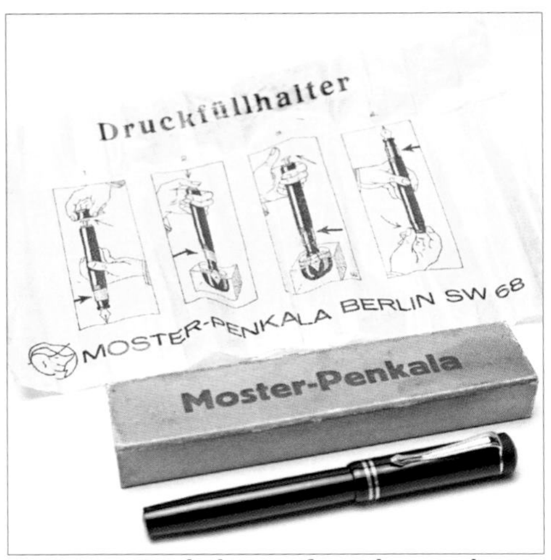

Moster-Penkala pen for sale on e-bay

Ser. No. 34,751. (CLASS 37. PAPER AND STATIONERY.) EDMUND MOSTER & Co., Zagreb, Hungary. Filed May 14, 1908.

Particular description of goods.—Automatic Lead-Pencils.

Trademark application: U.S. Patent Office Official Gazette, Volume 135, July 21, 1908, pg. 655.
Fun note: the PENKALA application appears next to the JELL-O application from Genesee Pure Food Company.

Greta and Karl on wedding day

Karl and Greta

Karl and his mother, Hermine

The Zionist Movement, the Haganah, and War of Independence

I heard about the Zionist movement when either Karl's name came up, or when my dad's mother, Gertrude Galson Greenberg (neé Maligson), discussed her time as a member of a youth group, "Blau-Weiss" in Germany, which in the 1920s became interested in the "Zionist movement."

Ever since the Romans destroyed the Second Temple in the 2nd century C.E. and scattered the Jewish people, the Jews of the diaspora desired to return to their historical homeland. Passover Seders have long included the phrase "next year in Jerusalem." During the late 19th century, in response to rising anti-Semitism in Europe. this vague desire coalesced into the Zionist movement, initially led by Theodore Herzl. This is the man that Buki's famous grandfather, Rabbi Alkalaj, supposedly inspired. In 1917 during WWI, Britain, partly to influence American and Russian support for the war, issued the Balfour Declaration which endorsed a national home for Jews in Palestine. At the end of the war, the Ottoman Empire was partitioned by Britain and France. Britain took control of Palestine. The influx of Jews to Palestine increased over the next twenty years. Resentment rose amongst the Arab residents, and intermittent violence broke out. Britain changed position several times on how many Jews could enter, and what form such a homeland might take. Realizing the importance of Arab oil, the British issued a White Paper in 1939 that limited Jewish emigration to 75,000 over five years and defined a joint Jewish-Arab control of Palestine. Both Jewish and Arab leaders rejected it.

When WWII came to an end, hundreds of thousands of Jewish refugees headed for Palestine. Britain, however, was only allowing a limited number to immigrate there, so most had to be smuggled in. In 1919, the Jewish population was 100,00. By the end of WWII in 1945, it had increased to 600,000.

Karl, fourth from left, as a trainer in the Haganah

As the scope and horror of the Holocaust became clear, support for a Jewish state increased. In 1947, the United Nations passed the resolution that recommended Palestine divide into separate Jewish and Arab states. Violence increased rapidly and escalated into a civil war. When Israel declared itself an independent state in May 1948, the civil war expanded into an invasion by five neighboring Arab nations. Israel won the war (The War of Independence) and by November a ceasefire was established, followed by armistice agreements in 1949.

Karl's involvement with the Haganah ended around the time he reconnected with Greta. Haganah in Hebrew means defense. The Haganah (1920-1948) was a defense against Palestinian Arabs combating Jewish settlers. They were not well armed but were effective. My mother's recollection is that Karl left the Haganah because of an action where Haganah soldiers were "shooting at each other." She is most likely referring to the conflict between the Haganah and the Irgun. The Irgun was a right-wing splinter group of the Haganah that advocated more violent methods. Some have referred to the Irgun as a terrorist organization. There were intermittent conflicts between the two groups, though eventually they coalesced into the Israeli Defense Force. Menachem Begin, who led the Irgun in 1944, later formed the right-wing Likud party, and eventually became prime minister in 1977.

Mom also notes, "Well, he (Karl) also didn't like crawling under barbed wire."

The Kinderheim

Neveh Hayeled, a children's home (kinderheim), in Nahariya, Israel

Greta went back to work, finding a job at a factory, replacing worn out shirt collars. My mom needed to continue her education. My mom's Uncle Bruno, Erna's husband, was a religious man and recommended a religious school for girls. My mother shares this story about this first school:

> *It seems I was always running from schools. I did not like this school. One day, I ran away. There was a very long road back to Tel Aviv. Along the way, there was a candy shop, where I stopped to buy some candy. This is where my mother found me. After that, I went to the boarding house in Nahariya, where I was much happier.*

My mom was unhappy at this religious school, but Greta needed a safe place for her daughter. The "Kinderheim," German for "Children's home," was recommended by Karl's ex-wife Nadija, with whom he remained friendly, though they had no children together. One thought was that this school would also help my mom assimilate with the culture and language of Palestine. So, in 1946, my mom moved to the kinderheim named Neveh Hayeled. It was a well-respected children's home located in Nahariya, on the northern coast of Israel. Nahariya is just 10 minutes from the border with Lebanon and today a two-hour drive from Tel Aviv, though in the 1940s by bus a much longer drive on smaller roads.

My mother registered at the kinderheim as Jehudit Alkalay. She has "very fond memories" of the two years she lived at the kinderheim.[8] At first, she missed her mother, but once she understood the routine, she relaxed and valued her time there. The kinderheim was a beautiful large house situated on a sandy beach by the Mediterranean Sea. It was run by a progressive German woman, Berta Hirsch, with her daughter Ester and Gershon De Haas. About fifty children lived there. The boys slept

8 I read of two WWII survivors who mentioned that on their arrival in Palestine, they went to live at Neveh Hayeled. Both were there at the same time as my mother. Henry Fenichel, who took the photo of the home at the head of this section and the photo

Neveh Hayeled Children: Jehudit (my mom) 2nd row from top, starting at the teacher on left, she is the 6th student in (between the two boys standing above her). Photo taken by Henry Fenichel, on display in Nahariya, Israel

upstairs, and the girls slept downstairs. The boys were taught skills such as woodworking, while the girls learned to manage the laundry, sew, prepare lunches for school, and to mend socks (the latter a skill my mom still finds useful when repairing socks that she has knitted and worn through).

Mom likes to tell a few vignettes of her time at the kinderheim. With a smile on her face she remembers the boys tearing sheets into strips, tying them together, making knots along the rope of sheets, and lowering themselves down to visit the girls. She explains:

> *It was nice to have their company. Most likely the adults were aware of what the boys were up to. I suspect the boys got their strength for climbing up and down those ropes because the school's teacher Gershon, in his previous life, before emigrating to Israel, was a gym teacher. Every morning, before starting school, he had the children run down to the beach, do exercises, go into the water, and run back to the house to get dressed for school. He was strict to the point of knocking on your arms to move them to the correct angle. It helped that he was a very handsome man!*

She enjoyed this routine and credits her youthful strength to this morning regimen. Thankfully, she didn't require her own children to rise early for exercise before school, although I personally got some exercise chasing after the school bus on a regular basis.

In other memories, chocolate and cookies come into play. We probably all have a childhood memory about candy or sweets. I used to go across the street, ring the doorbell of a friendly older woman with white hair, and be presented with a strip of paper on which rows of pink, yellow, and blue little sugar dots were waiting to be peeled off by tiny fingers and dissolved in the mouth. Here are some of my mother's candy and cookie stories:

My bedroom was in the hallway really, the passageway to other rooms. Some older girls were in a different room, a real room. Every night one of them read stories that I now realize were from comic strips. The entrance fee was a cookie, or just being liked by one of the older girls.

Every Friday, I was at the bus stop in Nahariya, waiting with a friend for the bus from Tel Aviv, not knowing if this Friday my mother would come to visit. On days my mother did not arrive, I would go with my friend to visit a distant relative of Karl's. If we hung around long enough, sometimes for several hours, this relative would eventually, reluctantly, offer us cookies. At some point, she caught on to our little plan and complained to Karl.

The kinderheim arranged work experiences for each child, appropriate to their age. My mother was assigned to an English woman who lived next door. Her task was to pull weeds, a job she did not enjoy. There is frustration in her voice as she remembers that she had to share her payment of chocolate with the other children at the kinderheim: "I always tried to hide a little extra for myself." This behavior of stashing a bit for herself still occurs as an adult. She cleverly hides from the view of her children, their spouses, and all her grandchildren, her current favorite candy, such as dark chocolate Kit Kat bars.

The children at the boarding house attended school in the village of Nahariya. Due to the war, my mom had lost some educational time, plus she did not know the language, so she was placed a year behind for her age. The children from the kinderheim befriended the village children. The lunches the kinderheim children brought to school were, as my mother explains:

...awful sandwiches. Bread smeared with chocolate from a jar given to them by the American Army. The town kids loved the chocolate bread. We traded our sandwiches for their cheese and tomato sandwiches. I loved their sandwiches. Unfortunately, the town parents weren't happy and complained.

Berta Hirsch, who ran the kinderheim, was quite interesting, playful and liberal in her ways. Mom remembers a large array of fancy theatrical outfits available for Purim:

Mom on the left

We had to dress up for Purim and go to the village with the local kids. I didn't know what I wanted to be, but the last two costumes in the trunk were these rococo dresses, which my Yeminite friend and I were told to wear. I thought I looked horrible and didn't want to go to the village. I drew a beauty mark on my face.
Now I think I look cute.

There was more going on in Nahariya beyond the day-to-day of living at the kinderheim and going to school. On the beaches of Nahariya, illegal immigrants were entering Israel. Some of these immigrants were hidden at the kinderheim:

We were told these people would be hidden under our beds and when the British soldiers came to search we must not say anything. It was a secret and it was all we could do not to laugh from fear and from nervousness.

In this quote, she reminds us that, when we are scared or see something bad happen, we sometimes laugh to reduce stress.

On December 14, 1945, the last of eight vessels carrying illegal immigrants, the Hannah Senesh, left Savona, Italy with 252 immigrants and arrived on Christmas Eve 1945, at a beach in Nahariya. The passengers were brought to shore by a rope bridge, evading capture. The name of this boat, Hannah Senesh, was named after a well-known poet, a parachutist who was killed by the Nazis in Yugoslavia in 1944.

Below is a photo of my mother standing on the beach at the Neveh Hayeled. Behind them, floating in the water, is the Hannah Senesh.

Mom, friend of Karl's, and Greta. The Neveh Hayeled made clothes for the children. They were given a choice of skirts. These photos show my mom in her choice of the pleated grey skirt and the red shirt.

Teenage Years

At this point, my mother has been introduced to many languages. She speaks Croatian with her mother. She hears her mother speaking Hungarian to her Hungarian friends and relatives. She uses Croatian or German with Karl and his mother. She learned Italian on Korčula and in Bari, English from the Americans, and then Hebrew in Israel. In the Israeli schools she studies French. This all leads to some communication difficulties between herself and her mom.

Mom spent two or three years at the kinderheim. When Karl and Greta married, my mom moved back to Tel Aviv to live with her mother and stepfather. In Tel Aviv, she attended an elementary school called, Beit Sefer Ledugmano (Le-Dugmah), which was a model school attached to the Women Teachers' Seminary. She recalls:

Classmates at the elementary school,
mom is taller because she is also a year older.

Dancing at school Beit Sefer Ledugmano, Tel Aviv, Mom 2nd from left.

Mom at the beach with friends

Mom leaning on a friend's motorcycle

> Beit Sefer Ledugmano *was a wonderful school, right by the beach. Mr. Dinitzky was my homeroom teacher. He taught Hebrew and another subject and helped with schoolwork after school. He was incredibly encouraging. He recommended I compete for a scholarship, which was an exam after 8th grade. At the time, families had to pay for high school. With this scholarship, I could go to high school at an exemplary school for free or I could get a stipend for a private school. Mr. Dinitzky and my friend and neighbor, Eitan who took the exam the year before, helped me study for the exam. I succeeded in receiving the scholarship. I chose the private school, Geula. That is when my studies really took off.*

Interestingly, a very close friend she met many years later, in Syracuse, New York, Varda Holland, also attended Geula high school, but not during the same years. They enjoy sharing memories.

Tel Aviv was where she finally settled into a period of life, such that, if you ask, "Since you lived in so many places, where do you feel you're from?," her response is "Tel Aviv, Israel." She had friends and boyfriends. The beach was a favorite meeting place. There were books to discover at the hole-in-the wall library she frequented.

Yet, terrorist activities and war marred what was otherwise a happy time. How did the wars in Israel affect my mother? She remembers filling sandbags to surround her building and protect the basement apartment where they would hide during air raids. The owner of the apartment building was Mrs. Eisenberg. A neighbor and friend Eitan[9] joined them in the air raid shelter because his home was only one story and not air raid safe. One time, mom worried about Karl, as he stood on the balcony, watching the bombing of Tel Aviv:

9 Eitan became a Professor and spent a summer visiting mom while studying at Syracuse University, accompanied by his wife and daughter.

Air raid and shooting sounds were scary. People were uptight. With knots in your stomach, you sat and waited for the all-clear siren. And, then you would get on with your life. As awful as it is to say, you felt lucky it wasn't you. The sounds never really disappear. I remember once [years later], when we lived across from an orchard, I heard a sound and said to Allen, a plane is going down. Sure enough, it was reported that a plane crashed in the orchards. Another time, I was walking along the sidewalk with colleagues. When I heard what sounded like gun shots, I instinctively jumped into the bushes. My boss exclaimed, "What happened to Nirelle?" and then suggested it was a car backfiring. The next day, it was reported in the papers that there was a shooting at the bus station we had been walking past.

Another way the war affected my mom is her tendency to hoard:

My mother (Greta) would buy fabric because it might run out and she would stock up on other supplies. Now I feel the need to hoard supplies just in case there isn't enough.

Growing up, we always had a well-stocked kitchen. My parents were stocked and prepared for Y2K. They are ready for storms and today, during the Covid-19 epidemic, my mom has bought supplies to last for months. In addition to hoarding, no food is wasted. Their refrigerator is full of little bits of food so as not to waste the last bite.

And sadly, she is impacted by the distant trauma of war in her dreams.

All kinds of fears you try to fight off. There are bad dreams about getting separated or meeting my father. There have been times when I'm screaming, and Allen has woken me.

Greta, Karl, and my mom

Pre-army or youth corps training started in Israel after the eighth grade. The trainers were only a few years older than my mom. They met once a week before the school day started. Here are my mother's thoughts on this training:

I don't believe in killing, but I did enjoy pre-army training. We were taught to clean guns, how to take them apart, how to climb under barbed wire, how to read topography, to not to take your high boots off in the sand, how to go arm over arm with ropes across rivers. One of my neighbors had trouble with all that and they let me carry her bags. They didn't like it, but they let me do it.

My mom, standing at the top of the pyramid. Pre-Army training.

ENGLAND

My mother was approaching the age when she would have to serve in the Israeli army. Consequently, the family sent her to Greta's sister, Ida, who was living in London, England. In London, she took courses at the London County Council College and later entered a secretarial college for women, Denson Laney School for Ladies. The stories of my mom's "escapes" from schools continues in England in the form of visiting boys after hours. One boy she visited, was David Kalderon:

I met David Kalderon on a bus to visit my cousin, Nandi, in Nahariya, Israel. David and I started dating and he even wanted to marry me. In England, I was still dating David. I complained to him, that I never met any of his friends. So, one day he invited me to come watch him play tennis with his friend, an American named Allen.

Allen Galson, was in London, England for a year, on a Fulbright Scholarship. He originally intended to study metallurgy in Sheffield. My dad, explains why he changed the location from Sheffield to London like this:

My girlfriend, at the time, informed me that there was no way she was going to live with me in boring old Sheffield. So, I convinced the Fullbright organization to send me instead to the Imperial College in London. Apparently, that was not enough for my snooty girlfriend, and she broke up with me anyway.

David Kalderon and Nirelle, London

In London, my dad moved into a two-bedroom flat with David Kalderon and began his studies in September 1953. He also began dating a German au pair who lived next door. Sometime during the Fall, my dad meets my mom while playing tennis with David. My mom begins to drop by the flat on a friendly basis to visit them. Over Christmas break, my dad and the German girlfriend went skiing in Austria, stopping to visit her family along the way.

When my dad returned from this adventure, he found a letter from the American Embassy, requesting that he immediately report to the Embassy with his passport. When he did, they took his passport and informed him that he would not be allowed to travel outside the UK other than to return home to the United States. The Consul read him a letter citing that he was accused of being a communist. The McCarthy era was in full swing and dad was swept up in the furor. Panicked, he and his family quickly moved to clear his name.

The accusation arose from his freshman year, when he was president of the Cornell chapter of the World Government Organization. My dad continues his story:

> *The chapter was committed to admitting anyone who supported its agenda, including Communist; it was heavily "infiltrated" by them. I became their unwitting front man. Someone at Cornell had "named names" to the FBI, and one of the names was Allen. Fortunately, we were able to quickly gather a number of influential people to attest to my good qualities. Key among these was a powerful Bronx congressman, whose sons had roomed with me at Cornell. He did not want a scandal coming anywhere near him and his family. By February my name was cleared and eventually my passport was returned.*

At the same time, because he was friendly with my mother, she was also investigated. My mom explains:

> *Amazingly, the FBI knew that I had been in a youth group in Israel. It was called, Hashomer Hatzair. Our teacher Mr. Vinitzki required us to join a youth group, so from the age of 14-16 I was a member of a group. I had no idea it was left leaning, but the FBI knew. I simply chose this group because it was in walking distance to my house. I enjoyed it because we went on excursions and learned how to be a cohesive group, working together. I guess they were kind of socialist in their ways.*

In fact, the Hashomer Hatzair youth group was a secular, socialist-zionist youth group which has become an international youth group today.

Alas, spring arrived, and this young man's fancy turned to...Nirelle. They began dating, went on some trips, and within a month they became engaged. My mom also had four other standing invitations to marry! Let's say, she likes to shop for the best deal, even today. She will research a purchase and wait for the best price. That isn't to say that impulse buying doesn't happen too, it does. Saying yes to my dad seems to be a combination of research and impulse for the best guy available.

In Britain, a girl could marry at age 16, but needed parental consent until the age of 21. Thus, mom, at the age of 19, needed permission from her mother to marry. The request was sent to Greta in Israel who called her sister Ida in London to discuss the qualities of Allen. Ida vouched for my dad and permission to marry was sent via telegram! Fun side note: Until 2012, Marriages had to be performed between 8am and 6pm.

In spring of 1954, my dad's Fulbright year was up and his funds depleted. He would need to return to the States soon. He went back to the American embassy to ask how he could bring his Israeli fiancée home to America. Given her association with a socialist, possibly communist leaning youth group, best to get married, he was told. So, ten days later, with a lot of scrambling, they got married!

It turns out, that my mom needed a plan too. From her Israeli passport we see that her stay in England was extended several times. The last extension was until Feb. 1954 and had not been renewed. By now, she had been in England for about two years. Yet, at this moment, she was staying in England as an illegal immigrant!

Nirelle and Allen on their wedding day,
London, June 21, 1954

Their wedding was witnessed by Greta's sister, Aunt Ida, and Allen's great uncle, Bernard Danneman (his grandmother Dora's brother).

Shortly after, they traveled to Paris for a week, and then on to Marseille. There, some urgently needed funds were wired from home, and they were able to proceed to Israel, and to Nirelle's family.

In Israel, they had hoped to have a Jewish wedding, but things didn't go so well, as mom explains:

> *In Israel, we wanted to have a wedding. We had a problem though. Dad could not easily prove he was Jewish! He had a letter from the rabbi his family knew well (in Syracuse). This rabbi was a reformed rabbi and therefore in the eyes of the rabbinate, not a rabbi at all. Your dad was offended and offered to lower his pants, but that only made them angry. So that did not work either and we scrapped the idea of a wedding and had a party.*

My sister, Deborah, recalls that during her visit to Israel she visited family members and all fondly remembered our parent's wedding party. They told her that Greta and Karl were known for their wonderful parties which they hosted on the roof of their apartment building, in Deb's words, "Greta and Karl liked to act things out. When they planned a party it was a big deal!"

My dad wrote how each of them arrived in New York City. These are his words:

After a month, Allen left for home, and when his ship arrived at the dock in New York, his waiting father had to pay some additional money to get the now bankrupt Allen and his luggage off the ship.

Meanwhile, Nirelle stayed in Israel to visit, and to convince the army to let her out of her required service. She put on a full charm offensive to a key bureaucrat and got her case put to the front of the queue. After three months, she was on a ship, and soon reunited with her new husband in New York.

Allen arrived on a small frieghter in New York, his dad had to pay to get him off the boat. This boat was sold to Argentina, then sunk.

Nirelle arrived by boat, the *Andrea Doria*, Manhatten New York, 1954. This boat collided with the *Stockholm* and sunk in 1956.

UNITED STATES

Allen and Nirelle

After visiting with their Syracuse family, Allen and Nirelle headed to Schenectady, New York where Allen had a job with GE. They spent about a year in Schenectady and then GE moved Allen's group to San Jose, California. Before they moved though, my dad encouraged my mom to attend college. She needed a high school diploma, which New York State granted her. Of this my mom states, "I was delighted! I always regretted not having a high school diploma."

Allen and Nirelle

Russel Sage College enrolled her with two years of college credit. Before she could take advantage of this opportunity, they moved to California with GE. In California, her experience did not go as far. My mom says with a laugh:

> *"I attended San Jose State. I wasn't given any credits. I had to start from scratch. I was required to take English for foreign students and Shakespeare."*

My mom and dad bought a house in Los Gatos. The house was purchased with the help of my mother's father, Buki. It is bittersweet that Buki is sadly not alive to see his daughter married, yet he is still able to help the newlyweds start a life together. As mentioned, Buki had sent some furs to a friend in NYC. Through the sale of these fur coats, Buki has given his daughter a wedding gift.

Their three children Deborah, Daniel, and Elizabeth (this author) were all born in California.

In 1961 the family moved back east to Syracuse, New York. Allen worked with his father and brother, Edgar at Galson and Galson Engineers. His mother, Gertrude worked for the firm as well, and later Edgar's wife joined Galson Technical Services. Nirelle raised a family, finished her college education at Syracuse University, and then worked for the university.

No. 7739342

Name GALSON, Nirelle Judith

residing at 16360 Los Gatos-Almaden Rd. Los Gatos, Cal

Date of birth Jun 10, 1935 Date of order of admission JUL - 1 1958

Date certificate issued JUL - 1 1958 by the

U. S. District Court at San Francisco, California

Petition No. 132742 Alien Registration No. 8 752 403

lm

Nirelle Judith Galson

(COMPLETE AND TRUE SIGNATURE OF HOLDER)

Nirelle Judith Galson
U.S. Naturalization Document, July 1, 1958

My mom, Deborah, Daniel, and Elizabeth, in the yard of their home on Los Gatos-Almaden Rd, Los Gatos, CA

EPILOGUE

HONORING THEIR LIFE TOGETHER as a married couple of fifty years, in 2004, my parents finally had the Jewish wedding they desired in 1954. Held in the backyard of their home at 5717 Thompson Road, in Syracuse, New York, under their majestic willow tree, friends and family enjoyed witnessing their union.

Holding chuppah (previously used at Deborah and Philip's wedding)
Left to Right:
Ilana, Brian, Sam, Zack
Grandma Gertrude (Allen's Mother) sitting in wheelchair, 100 years old
Officiating: Neal Hoffman

REFLECTIONS

"She saved my Life:"

Nirelle and her mother shared a bond, as mother and daughter might, moving through difficult years as my mom grew to adulthood during war times and conflicts. They also had mother-daughter disagreements and the distance of being worlds apart, where letter writing was the main means for communication and the occasional phone calls. The more I interviewed my mother for this work, the more I heard when she spoke about Greta, a mantra from her heart, "*She saved my life.*"

And, of her father: "*My dad is never far from my thoughts*," a direct quote from her bio statement for our family yearbook.

Return to Zagreb:

Mom shares a memory of Greta's retelling of a visit to Zagreb, after the war. Greta walked by the apartment they used to live in. She saw a woman on the balcony cleaning the rug she and Buki owned. It was jolting to see. Makes me tear up just thinking about it myself.

Gratitude:

I am so impressed and proud of my mother. She is beautiful, intelligent, fun, caring, gifted with languages, knowledgeable about every endeavor that crosses her path, be it about engineering, science, art, music, cuisine, oriental rugs, weaving, batik, knitting, the list is so long. She helped give us kids a rich and interesting life with foreign students and foreign foods at our home. She was a role model for many. She came to know a new country, raised a family while obtaining college degrees and working part time, had a long successful career and actively volunteered in not-for-profit organizations. I had the pleasure of attending her farewell from the Syracuse University Department of International Programs Abroad (DIPA), where she served as Executive Director for over thirty years. Her tenure included the 1988 terrorist attack of Pan Am 103 which exploded over Lockerbie, Scotland killing all passengers, including 35 of her students enrolled in a semester abroad. She grew the DIPA program from a few hundred to over several thousand students by improving the student experience abroad and establishing programs in new countries including China and Zimbabwe. Her staff sat in a large circle and each gave a story of how my mother impacted their lives, from patience to learning their jobs, to saving their lives. Now she enjoys retirement, keeping in touch with her grandchildren, and staying active and engaged in life. That's my mom. It has been quite a journey for little Djurdjica.

Future Stories:

Inevitably more memories and stories will be shared by my mom. For example, today I learned that my mom was fired from her job with the neighbor at the kinderheim. Laughing, she explained, "This person had the most beautiful pansies with the sweetest faces. They were really the most beautiful flowers I'd ever seen. I picked one of every color and dried them between the pages of a book. For this, I was fired." It has been a wonderful journey with my mother and father as we listened to stories, looked over photos, e-mailed questions, researched and edited together. I know our family will continue to hear more stories, which I hope to continue collecting for a supplement of vignettes.

AFTERWORD

WE ARE THREE SIBLINGS: Deborah (me), Daniel, and Elizabeth (Betsy). Our Mom has had an interesting life in very many ways, but her childhood was both fascinating and an enigma for a long time.

Growing up as the eldest child of a holocaust survivor made its mark on me even though Mom wouldn't really talk about her experiences as a Jewish Yugoslav child during WWII. Even her teen years after her arrival in Israel in 1945 were not reported to us in much detail while we were growing up. I knew the barest outline of her story, including that they were arrested from a train and jailed for some weeks before mysteriously being released, that her father died in WWII after he saved Mom and her mother by sending them to Italian-held territory posing as the family of a Turkish man. I was an avid reader as a child and in my teen years became immersed in reading books about Jewish experiences during the Holocaust and the establishment of the state of Israel at a time when none of this was mentioned in regular school and we did not attend religious school (although Mom taught Hebrew for several years). Holocaust literature told of many horrible things that were done, and I wondered about why I couldn't stop reading these books. Over time, I realized that I was looking to the heroes, those that fought back in a variety of ways, small and large, and wondering if I would have been one of them if I was faced with their situations. It was part of the reason that I planned to move to Israel after college and only applied to graduate schools in Israel. I did become a student at the Weizmann Institute, but I eventually returned to the US for the age-old reason – a fella.

When I transferred to Brandeis University to complete my graduate studies, I learned that "survivor guilt" was very common to first-born children of holocaust survivors. Understanding that and talking about those feelings with others helped me understand my feelings about the Holocaust. My peers and I discussed how we felt the burden of guilt that some of our parents felt about surviving the war. We wondered if we were in a concentration camp would we have survived the traumatic experience. Would we have shared our bits of bread with others starving? How would we have handled ourselves? Would we have been courageous? Would we have been heroes? Would we have risked our lives to save others? Our education in school about the holocaust was either non-existent or focused on the victims and the tragedies. We found ourselves yearning to hear stories of resistance and survival.

As my children learned about the holocaust, I recognized a similar set of feelings in them. My oldest, Zachary was overwhelmed by the stories of victimization. A few years later, my daughter Rebecca took a class through the gifted program where they read books and discussed the holocaust, focusing on both the victims and the heroes. It is hard to imagine such a tragedy as a holocaust. It is hard to believe it still happens. A counter balance of heroes and stories of the righteous helps us believe that people can overcome evil.

The other gap that I felt strongly as a young adult was that the message was that there was something terribly wrong with the Germans and that it could never happen here..... Little of the education about the holocaust really has focused on how a place where the Jews felt the most accepted and integrated (like here in the US) could flip so drastically so rapidly and how the normal institutions were subverted by the Nazis. This leads to complacency and lack of awareness of how social and political institutions start the process of such a flip, and how urgent it is to recognize these early steps and act to prevent their continuation. This, of course, does not only apply to Jews. And so the world has continued to see one holocaust after another happen in one form or another with the refrain that no one saw it coming...

I asked Mom many questions in the early years about her life, but she really wasn't ready to talk about much of it when I was asking – her response was generally that she didn't remember much because she was so young – and I eventually stopped asking. Even her stories about her years in Israel did not include many important details. I learned a few more stories from our Grandmother, who lived in Israel, but they were also only snippets. I didn't even know how much I didn't know and so didn't ask the right questions! Many years later, Mom took a writing class for fun and started writing some short stories about her childhood experiences. Slowly she has opened up more. However, it really took my sister Betsy deciding to dig in over the past few years and work with Mom to get enough information that she and her husband Paul could do a literal trip down memory lane from Zagreb, where our Mom was born, through her escape route that led to Sarejevo (the city of her father's family), and eventually ended up with her and her mother on the island of Korčula, then held by the Italians. Mom's story then takes her to Italy, Israel, England (where she married our Dad!), and eventually the US. Mom has had many first names across these moves, so when traveling as a young adult to visit family in different countries, my sibs and I always had to try out several names before the recognition and welcome came! Nirelle? Who? Ah, Djurdica in European countries and Judit in Israel. The details, stories, and photos that Betsy has managed to put together in this book tell the amazing early story of this woman who is our Mom. I'm so glad to finally know more about her early years (unjumbling much of our early bits of information!) and about other members of our family lost to us in time. I'm very grateful for all the hard work that my sister has put into this effort to pull our Mom's story together for us and for our kids and grandkids, etc. This book does not go into the absolutely amazing and inspiring adult life that our Mom has lead, so clearly a sequel is necessary!

With Love,
Deb Galson

NOTES

1. Languages

Language within the area of the former Yugoslavia is complicated. While the languages spoken by Serbs, Croats, and Bosnians are nearly identical, there are variations that are strongly tied to ethnic identities. These differences were suppressed during times of political unification, and conversely, accentuated as political divisions grew. Thus, under the unified Yugoslavia after WWII, there was only one official language, Serbo-Croatian. Since the breakup, however, there are now officially three different languages: Serbian, Croatian, and Bosnian. Each emphasizes its own unique words, somewhat differing pronunciations, and even different alphabets.

For example, when Paul and I toured Sarajevo, we were driven down a street that made up the cease-fire line between the Bosnian Serbs and the Bosnian non-Serbs. On the Serb side the street name was in the Cyrillic alphabet, while on the non-Serb side, the same street name was spelled with the Latin alphabet.

Slovenia has yet another linguistic variation, Slovene, which has a lot of German and Italian mixed into the Slavic base. It is further divided into seven localized dialects. No wonder that Slovenians were found to have the best language skills in all of Europe.

2. Illegal Immigrants

Learning about Karl's involvement with the Haganah, and their attempts to stop the deportation of Jewish people entering as "illegal immigrants," connected me to my son Brian, who engaged in non-violent actions to stop deportation of illegal immigrants in the United States. The world continues to be a messy place.

3. More to Learn

I have written about the history of Palestine and the establishment of Israel. The reader might take it upon themselves to read more about this time period for a better understanding of how Israel was formed, the relationship between the Jewish state, the Arab neighbors, the Palestinians, and the history from then to now.

4. The Pressburger Family

For further reading about the Pressburger siblings please refer to "The Pressburgers" written by June Engel and Joyce Gutmann.

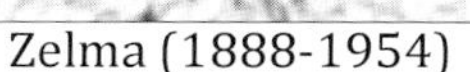
Zelma (1888-1954)

Ilona (1894-1984)

Frici (1896-1960)

Ida (1897-1984)

Sari (1899-1944)

Sabina (1901-1925)

Ilona, Ida, Greta (1903-1989) their grandmother, Janka Schwartz

Vilmos (c. 1893-1922)
no photo available

Hugo – died at Childbirth

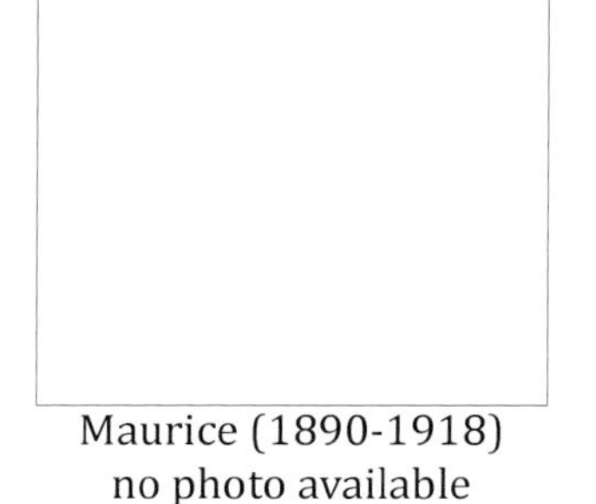
Maurice (1890-1918)
no photo available

Photo Gallery

Print

FEDERATIVNA NARODNA REPUBLIKA JUGOSLAVIJA
NARODNA REPUBLIKA HRVATSK

Kotar: Zagreb

Narodni odbor: ZAGREB, općina Donji grad

Očevid. broj: 1427 1956.

TAKSENA MARKA DIN 50

Izvod iz matične knjige rođenih

U matičnoj knjizi rođenih, koja se vodi kod ovog narodnog odbora za godinu 1935 na strani broj 12 pod rednim brojem 3 dana 10 mjeseca VI. godine 1935 upisan je:

Porodično i rođeno ime i spol djeteta:	Alkalaj Durdica (Nirelle)		
Dan, mjesec, godina i sat (0—24) rođenja: (ispisati i slovima)	10. (desetog) lipnja 1935.		
Mjesto rođenja, ulica i broj:	Zagreb		
Podaci o roditeljima	oca	majke	Naknadni upisi i bilješke:
Porodično ime (za majku i djevojačko)	Alkalaj	Presburger	
Rođeno ime	Buki	Greta	
Dan, mjesec i godina rođenja	—/—	—/—	
Mjesto rođenja	—/—	—/—	
Državljanstvo	—/—	—/—	
Narodnost	—/—	—/—	
Zanimanje	—/—	—/—	
Mjesto stanovanja	Zagreb		
Primjedbe i ispravci grješaka:	—/—		
Porodično i rođeno ime prijavitelja:	—/—		
Matičar:	—/—		

U Zagrebu

dne 24. VIII 1956.

M. P.

M. Bobetić
matičar

Zagrebačko knjižarsko poduzeće — T. 6331-55

Obr. IV-6

Birth certificate, Durdica Alkalaj,
June 10, 1935, Zagreb

Passport photo

Foreground: mom in arms of Aunt Sida, Buki's sister, Pre-WWII

Mom in Nahariya

Mom on left, Greta center and two cousins

Greta, Mom, Karl

Greta and Karl

Pre-Army training drills

Postcard drawn by Amnon Katz, of mom depicted holding her gun. He was her boyfriend at the time. He was in the army. They dated and socialized with a small group of friends, "He was gorgeous, with green eyes." Amnon moved to England as mom and dad went to Israel.

Mom at center with Amnon, artist of cat drawing, and friends

Naomi Laufer, best friend in Israel. Her father, Richard Laufer, known as, Rafael Rila, was a painter. We own two of his paintings.

Vally Engel (Raul's mother), Lizbeth Buchler (a second cousin*), Ellie (Zelma's daughter), Joyce (Frieda's daughter), Ida Pressburger, Nirelle, Frieda, Philip Buchler, Raul Engel (husband of June-Frieda's daughter. At Buchler home, London *Nirelle's grandmother, Rosalia had a sister, Theresa. Therasa's granddaughter is Lizbeth.

Nirelle, wearing a fur by Buki, cousin Joyce, and a friend traveling with Joyce at a beach in California.

Zelma's son, Nandi's family.
L-R: my sister, Deb, Nandi's daughter Petra, his wife Terra, Nirelle, Nandi

Deb, Dan, & Betsy 2019

Karl and Greta, as I remember them, Syracuse, New York.

Dad & Mom

Bibliography

Sources of Information

General WWII History Info

http://www.thepeoplehistory.com/1942.html
https://en.wikipedia.org/wiki/1942_in_Germany
https://www.history.com/topics/world-war-ii/world-war-ii-history#&gid=ci0230e631201a26df&pid=franklin-d-roosevelt-with-winston-churchill

Yugoslavia

https://en.wikipedia.org/wiki/Invasion_of_Yugoslavia
https://www.britannica.com/place/Yugoslavia-former-federated-nation-1929-2003
https://en.wikipedia.org/wiki/Yugoslavia
https://en.wikipedia.org/wiki/The_Holocaust_in_the_Independent_State_of_Croatia
https://www.yadvashem.org/odot_pdf/Microsoft%20Word%20-%206379.pdf
https://commons.wikimedia.org/wiki/Atlas_of_Yugoslavia#/media/File:Axis_occupation_of_Yugoslavia,_1941-43.png

Romano, Jasa. *Jews of Yugoslavia 1941-1945 Victims of Genocide and Freedom Fighters.* (From the English summary in the book Jevreji Jugoslavie 1941-1945. Zrtve Genocida I Ucesnici Narodnosloodilckog Rata, Belgrade: Federation of Jewish Communities of Yugoslavia, 1980; pp. 573-590.)

Freidenreich, Harriet Pass. *The Jews of Yugoslavia, A Quest for Community*. The Jewish Publication Society of America, 1979.

Goldstein, Ivo. "*The Jews in Yugoslavia 1918-1941, Antisemitism and the Struggle for Equality.*," http://web.ceu.hu/jewishstudies/pdf/02_goldstein.pdf.

Carpi, Daniel. "*The Rescue of Jews in the Italian Zone of Occupied Croatia.*" Shoah Resource Center. www.yadvashem.org.

Buki and Greta

Buki's name at Holocaust Survivors and Victims Data Base: https://www.ushmm.org/online/hsv/person_view.php?PersonId=7516235
Phone Book 1938: https://actacroatica.com/en/personas?q=Alkalaj
Buki in Footnotes of Design: Reklamni_zavod_Imago_i_komercijalni_graf.pdf
Street Info Sarajevo: https://sarajevo.travel/en/things-to-do/zelenih-beretki/337

Buki's Store mentioned

Kovac, Iasta."*Sephardi from Vlaska Street*," Sefardi iz Vlaške ulice. http://www.makabijada.com/dopis/vlaska.htm18.11.2006

Buki's Store mentioned

Magaš, Lovorka. "*Advertising Images commercial design in Croatia 1920's*," "*Reklamni zavod Imago I komercijalni grafički dizajn u Hrvatskoj 1920ih.*"
Website:https://www.academia.edu/20030487/Reklamni_zavod_Imago_i_komercijalni_grafi%C4%8Dki_dizajn_u_Hrvatskoj_1920_ih_Advertising_Agency_Imago_and_Commercial_Graphic_Design_in_Croatia_in_1920s_Peristil_51_2008_99_118.

Buki's Ad Image:

Švob, Melita. "*Adriatic Sea-Jewish port of Salvages.*" Research and Documentation Centar, Zagreb.

Buki's Ad Newspaper:
Malioglasi, Slovenec. Stran 12. 3, novembra 1929.
Greta
District Court of Tel Aviv. *The Palestine Gazette.* Thursday, No. 1487 pg 357.11th April, 1946.
Marriage Certificate, Hungarian data base
Sylvio
FK Željezničar, The Valley of the Cups Legend. http://Fkzeljeznicar.ba/
"FC Željezničar Sarajevo."
https://en.wikipedia.org/wiki/FK_%C5%BDeljezni%C4%8Dar_Sarajevo
Jasenovac Camp No. IV – Leather Shop, "Logor Jasenovac broj IV – Kožara." Feb 9, 2012.
Sarajevo
Friedman, Francine. Writing for Survival: Letters of Sarajevo Jews Before Their Liquidation During WWII. *Nostalgia, Loss and Creativity in South-East Europe*. Chapter pp 189-212. https://link.springer.com/chapter/10.1007/978-3-319-71252-9_8
Destination Sarajevo. Zelenih Beretki Street.
Childhood early memory, Nirelle J. Galson, 2002
Jasenovac
https://jasenovac.org/what-was-jasenovac/
https://en.wikipedia.org/wiki/Jasenovac_concentration_camp
List of Victims: https://www.ushmm.org/online/hsv/source_view.php?SourceId=45409
Mostar
https://en.wikipedia.org/wiki/Mostar
Palmberger, Monika. *"Fragments of Communcative Memory: World War II,"* Tito and the *1992-95 War.* https://link.springer.com/chapter/10.1057/978-1-137-45063-0_2.
Split
https://www.jewishvirtuallibrary.org/split
https://en.wikipedia.org/wiki/Province_of_Spalato
"The Rescue of Jews in the Italian Zone of Occupied Croatia," Danel Carpi
https://www.yadvashem.org/odot_pdf/Microsoft%20Word%20-%204803.pdf
Steinberg, Jonathan (2002) All Or Nothing: The Axis and the Holocaust, 1941-1943, Routledge; ISBN 0-415-29069-4, pg. 34
Independent State of Croatia, NDH
https://simple.wikipedia.org/wiki/Independent_State_of_Croatia
Švob, Melita. *"Adriatic Sea-Jewish port of Salvages."* Research and Documentation Centar,Zagreb.
Korčula
Korčula Island camp (Italian zone)
Korčula Island maritime Zionist camp (Vela Luka)
Maritime Zionist camps
THE MAGIC TRUNK IN KORCHULA, Nirelle J. Galson, May 21, 2002
https://www.researchgate.net/publication/292673982_ESCAPE_FROM_THE_HOLOCAUST_YUGOSLAV_JEWS_IN_SWITZERLAND_1941-1945/fulltext/56b0ca3708ae9ea7c3b28785/ESCAPE-FROM-THE-HOLOCAUST-YUGOSLAV-JEWS-IN-SWITZERLAND-1941-1945.pdf
Flory Jagoda Interview:
https://collections.ushmm.org/search/catalog/irn504836

Bimba Beck Interview: https://kentuckyoralhistory.org/ark:/16417/xt7dv40jwq9t
Italy
https://en.wikipedia.org/wiki/The_Holocaust_in_Italy
https://www.britannica.com/place/Italy/End-of-the-regime
https://spartacus-educational.com/2WWitaly.htm
https://en.wikipedia.org/wiki/Allied_invasion_of_Italy
https://uca.edu/politicalscience/dadm-project/europerussiacentral-asia-region/yugoslavia-1918-2003/
Image of Refugee at Bari:
http://www.annapizzuti.it/database/ricerca.php?a=view&recid=147
Bari 2nd Pearl Harbor
BARI, ITALY (revised), Nirelle J. Galson, May 11, 2009
https://www.americanheritage.com/content/disaster-bari-0
Diseases
https://www.ncbi.nlm.nih.gov/pmc/articles/PMC5105226/
https://www.aapc.com/blog/26557-wwii-military-health-in-the-pacific/Flit
https://livinghistoryfarm.org/farminginthe40s/pests_01.html
Marlene
https://sistercelluloid.com/2014/12/27/a-soldier-lovingly-remembers-marlene-dietrich/
www.womenshistory.org/education-resources/biographies/marlene-dietrich.
The MUZAK project info from:
https://www.cia.gov/news-information/featured-story-archive/2008-featured-story-archive/marlene-dietrich.html
Family comment from, https://en.wikipedia.org/wiki/Marlene_Dietrich
Jewish Brigade
https://encyclopedia.ushmm.org/content/en/article/jewish-brigade-group
https://www.haaretz.com/israel-news/.premium-jewish-soldiers-who-fought-the-nazis-receive-italy-s-highest-military-honor-1.6529218
https://en.wikipedia.org/wiki/Jewish_Brigade
General Twining
https://www.af.mil/About-Us/Biographies/Display/Article/105367/general-nathan-f-twining/
Palestine-Israel
http://museum.rutkin.info/en/node/27
https://www.britannica.com/topic/Haganah
https://www.jewishvirtuallibrary.org/atlit-immigration-camp
https://encyclopedia.ushmm.org/content/en/article/postwar-refugee-crisis-and-the-establishment-of-the-state-of-israel
https://encyclopedia.1914-1918-online.net/article/british_mandate_for_palestine
https://www.jewishvirtuallibrary.org/background-and-overview-israel-war-of-independence
https://www.jewishvirtuallibrary.org/the-role-of-jewish-defense-organizations-in-palestine-1903-1948
https://www.britannica.com/event/Arab-Israeli-wars
https://jwa.org/encyclopedia/article/habas-bracha

Kochavi, Arieh J. "The Struggle against Jewish Immigration to Palestine." Middle Eastern Studies, vol. 34, no. 3, 1998, pp. 146–167. JSTOR, www.jstor.org/stable/4283956. Accessed 4 Jan. 2021.

Karl Moster

http://www.penkala.net/Penkala/penkala.html
https://en.wikipedia.org/wiki/Edmund_Moster
https://leaderssummit.medium.com/plight-of-croatias-jews-restitution-of-private-property-blocked-by-the-balkan-country-s-142b95c8dc51
https://babel.hathitrust.org/cgi/t?id=pst.000064089881&view=1up&seq=671&q1=moster
http://collection.mjhnyc.org/index.php?keywords=karl+moster
http://collection.mjhnyc.org/index.php?g=detail&action=search&object_id=16364

Kinderheim

http://genealogyindexer.org/view/1965Israel/1965Israel%20-%200605.pdf
https://de.wikipedia.org/wiki/J%C3%BCdisches_Landschulheim_Coburg Fenichel:
https://www.dutchnews.nl/features/2020/04/they-were-proud-of-what-they-were-doing-a-dutch-holocaust-survivors-story/
https://cincinnatijudaicafund.com/Detail/objects/344
https://www.nhs-cba.org/Hazak12-16-15Photos.htm